STEPHEN BOYD has led on economic and industr
2003. A regular media commentator, he sits on
task groups and is an Honorary Research Fellov

GEORGE KEREVAN is the SNP MP for East Lothian and a member of the UK Parliament's Treasury Select Committee. An economist by training, he taught economics at Napier University in Edinburgh before serving nine years as Associate Editor of *The Scotsman* newspaper, where he was chief leader writer. He is also a documentary film maker and was executive producer of 'The Fog of Strenrenica', which won the prestigious Special Jury award at the 2015 Amsterdam International Documentary Film Festival.

KATHERINE TREBECK is Senior Researcher for Oxfam GB. She has a PhD in political science from the ANU, is Honorary Professor at the University of the West of Scotland and Senior Visiting Research Fellow at the University of Strathclyde. When working for Oxfam Scotland, Katherine developed the Humankind Index, a measure of prosperity constructed through community consultation.

Open Scotland is a series which aims to open up debate about the future of Scotland and do this by challenging the closed nature of many conversations, assumptions and parts of society. It is based on the belief that the closed Scotland has to be understood, and that this is a prerequisite for the kind of debate and change society needs to have to challenge the status quo. It does this in a non-partisan, pluralist and open-minded manner, which contributes to making the idea of self-government into a genuine discussion about the prospects and possibilities of social change.

Luath Press is an independently owned and managed book publishing company based in Scotland, and is not aligned to any political party or grouping. *Viewpoints* is an occasional series exploring issues of current and future relevance.

Tackling Timorous Economics

How Scotland's Economy Could Work Better for Us All

KATHERINE TREBECK
GEORGE KEREVAN
STEPHEN BOYD

Luath Press Limited
EDINBURGH
www.luath.co.uk

First published 2017

ISBN: 978-1-910021-37-8

The paper used in this book is recyclable. It is made from
low chlorine pulps produced in a low energy, low emissions manner
from renewable forests.

Printed and bound by
Bell & Bain Ltd., Glasgow

Typeset in 11.5 point Sabon
by 3btype.com

Contents

Our Economic System is broken. We need a new one.

KATHERINE TREBECK

The true objective of our politics and economy

THIS IS A BOOK that worries that we seem to be taking the long route to attain what people and planet need. It is a book that suggests real progress boils down to the sustainable wellbeing of a society; it takes a multidimensional conception of the possibilities people have for leading a good life.[1] The first and foremost objective of progress is what people and planet need – as opposed to putting economic objectives before all else. In this sense, 'progress' and 'development' are not only about Gross Domestic Product (GDP), not merely profits, and certainly not exhausting the planet until it is too late.

So it is also a book about putting economics back in its place as servant of the people (rather than people being valued only as factors of production). It confronts the origins of unequal distribution of human wellbeing. It calls out the economic system as insufficiently configured to deliver real progress and instead too often operating so as to reward the powerful and give power to those with most rewards. It highlights that the wrong sort of growth can be harmful – more is not always good. And it recognises that the nature of economic growth as currently pursued may destroy the environment which is so important for economic and human wellbeing.

In recognising where things have gone awry and holding onto a sense of the extent to which things could be better, this book dives into the heightened possibility of one country – Scotland. Scotland has an economy shaped by a range of forces – political, global, geographical, cultural, historical, and technological. It can be a self-aware place poised for change and rich with potential.

It is an over-used cliché, but Scotland does stand at a crossroads. The UK vote to leave the European Union has created a state of suspension in that we know much will change, yet in what way and with what impact is far from clear. Already more powers are shifting to the Scottish Parliament, Holyrood; people are discussing what sort of country we want to be; and organisations and government are responding to this 'democratic renewal' by recognising the need to really engage communities, rather than just consult those who reply.

So in a way Scotland is the playground for the authors of the book to allow our ambitions for the country to clamber over and beyond the obstacles and hurdles of short term and constrained policy making. Scotland is the terrain in which this book seeks to envisage an economy that supports the real needs of people and planet, but the messages within are not for Scotland alone.

Where we are now

In developed countries such as Scotland, indications are that we are going beyond 'enough': we have passed the point of saturation. In 1989 Max-Neef pointed to a 'threshold', explaining that

> in every society there is a period in which economic growth contributes to an improvement of the quality of life, but only up to a point, the threshold point, beyond which if there is more economic growth, quality of life may begin to deteriorate.[2]

Quality of life deteriorates because after this point the costs of increasing GDP are higher than the wellbeing it provides; defensive expenditures become dominant and economic growth becomes uneconomic.[3] Demand for many services is driven by inequality and 'failure' to get things right in the first place.[4]

This is caused by and is simultaneously manifest in multiple crises – climate change, environmental destruction, inequality, alienation, and disengagement.

Yet the crisis the world's leaders (as opposed to people and communities) woke up to with most alertness was the financial crisis. To this the default response was to push down further on the accelerator and stoke the engine with more fuel. In other words, we got the opposite of the profound change of direction sorely needed.

Instead, according to recent analysis from the Office for Budget Responsibility, the UK economy is exhibiting many features of the pre-2008 style economy. There is no sign of the much vaunted 'rebalancing' (from finance to manufacturing, from consumption to investment, and from wealthier to poorer regions). In Scotland, like the UK as a whole, we have seen a recovery of financial and business services more rapid than in manufacturing (where at the time of writing output has yet to recover to pre-recession levels).

This pathway has seen a large majority of workers in Scotland experience a historically unprecedented decline in the real value of their wages between 2009 and 2014. But some occupations received *real terms* increases, namely corporate managers and directors.[5] Another indication of the extent to which the economy splinters people's economic standing, rather than supports it, is financial insecurity: according to the Centre for Social Justice, household debt is at a historic high of £1.47 trillion and 8.8 million people struggle with over-indebtedness.[6]

The long way around

This economic model represents an approach to progress and development that demands more resources, more effort, more political agreement, and more patience than need be. It is an inefficient approach to delivering good lives sustainably. And it is bumpier, has more distractions and diversions and flimsy bridges to cross than the route we could be taking.

At its simplest, this long way to good lives entails:

- Firstly, get the economy to grow bigger, but don't fret too much about the damage to people or the environment that this does

- Secondly, take a chunk out of this economy via taxes
- Thirdly, channel this money to helping people cope with step number 1

Step three is evident in symptoms such as: tax credits for those in jobs which do not pay enough to live on; interventionist medical treatment for those alienated and stressed by the precariousness of this economy; welfare payments for those cast aside by companies who downsize in their quest for short term shareholder value; and via flood defences and shelters for those whose homes are flooded as climate chaos worsens. All this provision is undeniably vitally important for recipients in the short term, but arguably it is also a sign of attempts to heal and ameliorate rather than prevent harm in the first place.

Essentially the long road is 'end of play' redistribution and putting sticking plasters over the wounds caused during the match. As Danny Dorling has warned, we cannot keep plastering over 'wounds caused by inequality by building more prisons, hiring more police and prescribing more drugs'.[7]

But we continue doing this because our current path is ostensibly unable to get the distribution right first time around, let alone creating healthy people and a sustainable planet. Globally, of all the income generated by GDP growth between 1999 and 2008, the poorest 60 per cent of humanity received only 5 per cent of it; the richest 40 per cent of people, by contrast, received 95 per cent.[8] 1.1 billion people live in extreme poverty – but the Overseas Development Institute has shown that this figure could have been reduced by 200 million if poor people had benefited equally from the proceeds of growth during the Millennium Development Goal period.[9]

Not only is a deluded reliance on trickle-down economics an incredibly inefficient pathway to poverty alleviation, it is environmentally unsustainable.[10] It depends on a growing economy which is dangerously pushing beyond planetary boundaries.[11] In many countries this growth is premised on exploiting natural resources and has been described as a 'neo-extractivist' model (Brazil's mega-projects in agriculture, oil, and mining; or the UK's North Sea oil come to mind as examples).[12]

And the current route to good lives is also flimsy – vulnerable to fleeting and flippant political will. It further depends on the consent of those being taxed – a consent undermined by the inequality that separates communities from each other and undermines solidarity across society.

This bears out Karl Polanyi's observation[13] of what he termed a 'Double Movement' – the inevitable reaction of society to the impact of the spread of market economy (the reaction comes in the form of protective labour, civic, social and political movements, and various legislation [public health, factory conditions, social insurance, public utilities, municipal services, and trade union rights]). Polanyi warned that as the consequences of unrestrained markets become obvious, like an elastic band there are two scenarios – either it snaps (social disintegration) or it reverts to its previous position (laissez faire is constrained).

Wouldn't it be better not to over-extend the elastic band in the first place?

Why we are where we are

Until Scotland allows itself to discard conventional wisdom and orthodox thinking – becomes more 'timorous' – and until it ceases unquestioning adoption of agendas and positions, it will struggle to benefit from a vigorous, nuanced, and ambitious discussion about the purpose and structure of the economy we sorely need.

There seems to be an 'intellectual uniform' prevalent in some parts of Scottish life: adoption of certain stances because of party membership or organisational affiliation. This can be seen in the (almost) hysteria that breaks out if someone dares to question 'universalism'. Rather than a steady, clever, and thoughtful conversation about *what* is provided from public funds on a universal basis, there is polarised and unhelpful outburst along the lines of all or nothing universalism – a false binary if ever there was. Groupthink can also be seen in the cry from some that all Scotland's problems stem from a neoliberal agenda imposed from outside. But not only is there a plausible argument that in fact, it is not neoliberalism we have had, but an 'assetisation';[14] there is also plenty that all levels of government in Scotland could do *now* to begin to build, cajole, and enhance a more people-focused economic model.

Seeking out the analysis of those more expert than us is one thing, but simplistically assuming an intellectual uniform means we come to rely on others for our positions, which leads to an unhealthy, if energetic, deference to groups (be they political parties or campaign groups or others). And within these narrow spaces people seem anxious not to be the first one to stop clapping – resulting in too much adulation and not nearly enough querying of the logic, insufficient probing of the consistency, and scant asking to see the whole picture. Even if there are several groups, it is still groupthink...

So we get an immaturity of discussion and hints of intolerance of diversity; somewhat like two year olds, just learning to walk, waddling about, bumping into each other, and beginning to wail. Instead we should be gently and thoughtfully negotiating our different positions, and maybe even holding hands at some stage.

But the prevailing mood and mode boxes us into positions. Boxes are never helpful – instead they are about containment; they simplify complexity and nuance; and they force us to focus on the symbolic rather than the substance. Just look at the criticism Scottish Labour faced back in 2014 when it worked with the Conservatives in the Better Together campaign (when the two put aside differences to focus on a shared goal). Or, the following year, when ill-fated Labour leader Ed Miliband suggested he might step away from government if government meant coalition with the Scottish National Party.

Unwillingness to work with opponents bodes badly no matter which party (if any) one gravitates towards: it undermines efforts to put aside party differences for the greater good (however that is defined) and blocks much needed deliberation and dialogue. This is hardly grown up politics, instead it entrenches tribalism rather than encouraging shared agendas. As Gerry Hassan observes, 'a proper debate involves being able to empathise with your opponent, to be able to understand them and better inform your own views'.[15]

A narrow terrain

But of course Scotland's deliberations (and efforts to position competitiveness and tackling inequality as 'mutually supportive goals')[16] operate in the context of another narrative: a narrow economic orthodoxy. This is perpetuated by the mainstream media, by most political parties (again with notable exceptions, often in the form of individuals within them), by establishment academia, and many funding bodies. This orthodoxy positions the 'Global race', the mantra of competitiveness, efficiency, and GDP growth as goals in themselves, rather than the sustainable wellbeing of our society. It focuses on ring-fencing down-stream spending (important though that might be in the short term) rather than a desperately needed shift to preventative investment. Anything outside this narrow bandwidth is dismissed as 'radical' or 'unrealistic' or 'naive'. As Zoe Williams has noted:

> This is the whole of British politics encapsulated in two lines: unless a policy looks exactly like what the mainstream parties are suggesting... unless it will leave the fundamental structures totally unperturbed – then it is the most outlandish idea that anybody has ever heard.[17]

Getting it right in the first place

This long way around (growth-based economic model) would be tolerable *if* economic growth (that is, ever-rising GDP) could be *recoupled with* poverty reduction and *decoupled from* environmental degradation.

But this is a big – nae a huge! – task.

So why not find other means to deliver what people and planet need? How about delivering our objectives of a more equal, more humane and more sustainable society in the first place, rather than constantly having to beg for resources to heal the damage done by a growth-first, long way round model?

Getting this right might mean a smaller police force – even a smaller NHS – because people are safe and healthy. Already. It would mean less tax being diverted to top up poverty wages because jobs pay enough to live on. In the first place.

Getting it right means creating an economy that does more of the heavy lifting: configuring our economy so it generates jobs that deliver basic needs like security and sufficiency of income, but also important psychological needs such as control, autonomy, self-esteem, and meaning. It means putting the objectives of good lives and greater equality at the very forefront of decision-making – rather than some rather unimpressive means to get there (you know who you are GDP).

This book

The authors in this book argue for greater attention to the *quality* of our economy and the three chapters offer a range of ideas to get there – necessary perhaps, but not sufficient. They are areas in which we urge experimentation – with Scotland as a laboratory made possible by, *inter alia*, the 2014 Scottish independence referendum which opened a popular (if imperfect) debate regarding new solutions to old economic problems.

Recommendations for change include:

The taxation we need

Taxation is an important lever to help shape the sort of society and economy we want:

- It can build in incentives so that managers take account of long term social and environmental goals[18]

- It can tax unearned good fortune[19]

- It can redistribute by ensuring the whole tax system is robust and progressive[20]

Stephen Boyd, for example, explains why increasing tax revenues as a proportion of GDP is necessary if anything close to Scandinavian levels of equality are to be achieved (with the tax take then used to fund the transfers that reduce inequality). But within a higher tax take Boyd also recommends raising the top rate of income tax – out of a recognition that high marginal tax rates may have indirect effects, especially on corporate behaviour, that are socially valuable.

George Kerevan reminds us that taxes on capital are an important tool in three senses: (1) taxes on profit streams; (2) taxes on capital gains; and (3) taxes on gross wealth itself. Kerevan also recommends taxing profits at a higher rate (rather than inputs such as labour and property). A global wealth tax would eliminate distortions in allocation between nations, as the same tax would prevail everywhere.

Shifting the tax burden to capital, wealth and harmful activities should be intuitive, yet governments often claim that doing so would lead to 'flight' of the 'wealth creators'. Leaving aside that 'trickle down economics' from such wealth creators has yet to prove itself, the reality is that the number of people who move for tax reasons is negligible, even amongst the wealthy (usually only a few celebrities). Another form of unearned wealth is that which gets handed down from one generation to another – so Boyd recommends a 'fair' level of inheritance tax. He warns: 'choose not to have a fair inheritance tax; deserve to have society run by the rentier class'.

Beyond tax: the economy we need

If we are to truly transform and lighten our impact on the planet we need to transform how we manufacture products and dramatically alter how we use them. In my chapter I suggest that part of this is about a shift from a take-make-waste linear business model to 'lease the resource, make the product, recover the resource and then remake it'.[21] Simultaneously, consumers need to be better at sharing capital goods (such as sharing cars, tools, or white goods). In other words, we need an economy that is circular and collaborative.

Boyd adds that it is necessary to develop a 'foundational'

economic strategy for Scotland which concentrates on 'mundane' economic sectors like supermarkets and other retail, utilities, transport, retail banking and the public sector where most people actually work. Such franchises underpin much economic activity and should be utilised to boost job numbers and quality.

This is a far cry from the deference to wealth that seems to characterise the current configuration of policy-making and economic decisions. As Boyd observes, growing the financial sector *as an end in itself* has been a consistent priority of *all administrations* since devolution.

The businesses we need

Currently businesses externalise many costs – one corporation's actions and assets become liabilities for other parties, such as taxpayers, businesses, families, and the ecosystem.[22] Behind this transfer of cost is an interpretation of fiduciary duty (many would say mistakenly) as a duty on corporate managers to maximise shareholder return (in the short term). As I argue in this book, such an interpretation means that social and environmental externalities (bad and good) are both over- and under-delivered.

Instead, businesses need to be driven by a sense of purpose to enhance communities and conserve the ecological systems where they operate. One mechanism would be to 're-purpose' businesses so they internalise costs currently seen as externalities and to imbue in private organisations a wider, more collectively orientated purpose (so they generate positive externalities). For example, ensuring company boards represent a range of constituencies could begin such re-purposing. But, there are other mechanisms beyond the board: employees and managers can be incentivised differently via long term value creation targets that determine reward and promotion; and new business models that democratise ownership. Employee and community cooperatives present a way to do business that is better aligned to the needs of people and planet, rather than simply profit.

As Kerevan highlights in his contribution, this is about democratising the market economy itself; providing broader access to productive resources and opportunities. Firms and factories managed by worker cooperatives decide what they produce, how they produce it, and what they charge for their products; while the incomes of all workers are profit shares, not wages.

The work we need

Within all enterprises, the way work is managed and controlled; the type of work; the pay and conditions of work; and the relationship workers have with each other, are all an opportunity for better alignment between the economy and what people want and need.

All three authors support what is perhaps the simplest immediate labour market intervention: to ensure every worker receives a living wage. However, given that the increase in inequality over the longer term has been driven more by runaway wage increases at the top end of the distribution rather than stagnating wages at the bottom, it is important not to claim too much for the impact of increasing the minimum wage or wider introduction of the living wage.

The amount of work is also a factor contributing to inequality: simultaneous over- and under-work suggests that better sharing the available work is needed. Both myself and Kerevan point to the Netherlands as a model for better sharing work.

The security we need

Support when people encounter misfortune – such as ill-health or unemployment – is crucial in underpinning a decent society, enabling the economy to function and ensuring people are secure. But much change explored in this book will only be facilitated by a shift away from the tyranny of short-termism which seems all too pervasive in both business and politics. Instead we need upstream, preventative spending (as opposed to 'failure demand'), connected polices, long term budgets, and enabling government departments to benefit from results that accrue down the line or in another department's balance sheet.

Scotland is gaining more control over various aspects of benefits – and of course already has control over the NHS. But recognising the interaction of the benefit system with the realities of the labour market is important.

The things we don't really need

My contribution points to the need to 'decouple aspiration from consumption' and to decouple remaining consumption from impact on the planet. The challenge is great given the manner in which our current economic model depends on people buying more and more products, and that inequality plays upon people's need for status. The more anxious people are about their status, the more consumption is seen as a means to assert a sought position in the socio-economic hierarchy. The very real human need to belong to and be esteemed by one's peer group is exploited by marketers in ways that encourage consumption.

Greater equality is thus important in breaking the link between status anxiety and consumption. But on the way there we need businesses to stop advertising in a way that turns wants into needs.

Measuring what we need

There is no shortage of research, writing and evidence highlighting the deficiency of GDP as a measure of economic, let alone societal, progress. My chapter speaks of how pursuit of GDP without equivalent or greater regard for other indicators of real progress is no longer improving people's lives in wealthy nations and is putting more and more pressure on the planet. We need to recognise that real development does not simply mean GDP growth (for example, in countries such as the UK and Australia suicide is the biggest cause of death for young men, but these are countries that presume to call themselves 'developed').

So we need new measures of progress. But in developing more appropriate measures, it is vital to take account of people's views, needs and preferences. Exclusively expert or elite authored measures are another form of elite capture and democratic deficit.

Getting what we need

The ideas and changes suggested in this book are merely a selection of those necessary, or indeed possible, in Scotland and elsewhere.

They come from writers and activists of different persuasions who retain healthy differences regarding the way forward for Scotland. Nevertheless these authors are united in their belief that social and economic experimentation is of the essence if new solutions are to be found. This requires that decision makers in politics support good policies rather than submitting to tribal political point scoring which puts the interest of parties ahead of that of the people. And it requires that decision makers everywhere put the needs of people and planet before pounds and profit.

Notes

1   See Smith and Max-Neef, 2011: 142 and Watkins, 2013
2   Smith and Max-Neef, 2011: 146
3   Smith and Max-Neef, 2011: 148
4   Christie Commission, 2011
5   Office for National Statistics, 2015
6   Centre for Social Justice, 2015
7   Dorling, 2010: 318
8   Hickel, 2015
9   Hardoon and Slater, 2015
10 Alexander, 2015
11 See Jackson, 2009 and Steffen *et al.*, 2015
12 Acosta, 2013
13 Polanyi Levitt, 2013: 16 and Fred Block in Polanyi, 1944 this edition 2001: xxv
14 Birch, 2015
15 http://www.dailyrecord.co.uk/news/politics/gerry-hassan-weve-managed-lose-5961027
16 Scottish Government, 2015
17 Williams, 2015
18 For example, more tax levied on these companies with extreme

earnings inequality or undertaking polluting activities; a lower rate for those activities which are sustainable and contribute to social goals.

19 Such as an inheritance or a windfall gain.

20 Including taxing wealth, the value of land, and capital more heavily than labour.

21 Thomas, 2012

22 Trucost, 2013

References

Acosta, Alberto (2013) 'Extractivism and neoextractivism:two sides of the same curse' in Lang, M & Mokrani, D (eds.) *Beyond Development: Alternative Visions from Latin America*. Quito: Transnational Institute and Rosa Luxemburg Foundation http://www.tni-books.org/books/26-beyond-development.html (downloaded 1 August 2014)

Alexander, Samuel (2015) 'Sustained economic growth: United Nations mistakes the poison for the cure' *The Conversation* [Online] https://theconversation.com/sustained-economic-growth-united-nations-mistakes-the-poison-for-the-cure-47691 (downloaded 26 December 2015)

Birch, Kean (2015) *We Have Never Been Neoliberal – A Manifestor for a Doomed Youth*, Arlesford: Zero Books

Centre for Social Justice (2015) 'Future Finance: A new approach to financial capability'. in Centre for Social Justice (ed.). London: http://www.centreforsocialjustice.org.uk/UserStorage/pdf/Pdf%20reports/CSJ---Future-Finance.pdf (downloaded 26 December 2015)

Christie Commission (2011) 'Commission on the Future Delivery of Public Services' in Scottish Government (ed.) Edinburgh www.scotland.gov.uk/Publications/2011/06/27154527/2 (downloaded 29 June 2011)

Dorling, Danny (2010) *Injustice: Why Social Inequality Persists*, Bristol: The Policy Press

Hardoon, Deborah & Slater, Jon (2015) 'Inequality and the End of Extreme Poverty' Oxfam GB (ed) Oxford http://policy-practice.oxfam.org.uk/publications/inequality-and-the-end-of-extreme-poverty-577506 (downloaded 26 December 2015)

Hickel, Jason (2015) 'It will take 100 years for the world's poorest people to earn $1.25 a day' *The Guardian*, London http://www.theguardian.com/global-development-professionals-network/2015/mar/30/it-will-take-100-years-for-the-worlds-poorest-people-to-earn-125-a-day (downloaded 26 December 2015)

Jackson, Tim (2009) 'Prosperity Without Growth? The Transition to a Sustainable Economy' Sustainable Development Commission: London http://www.sd-commission.org.uk/publications.php?id=914 (downloaded 8 July 2010)

Office for National Statistics (2015) 'Annual Survey of Hours and Earnings: 2014 Revised Results' Newport http://www.ons.gov.uk/ons/rel/ashe/annual-survey-of-hours-and-earnings/2014-revised-results/index.html (downloaded 26 December 2015)

Polanyi, Karl (1944: this edition 2001) *The Great Transformation – The Political and Economic Origins of Our Time*, Boston: Beacon Press

Polanyi Levitt, Kari (2013) *From the Great Transformation to the Great Financialisation: On Karl Polanyi and Other Essays*, Black Point: Fernwood Publishing

Scottish Government (2015) 'Scotland's Economic Strategy' Edinburgh http://www.gov.scot/Publications/2015/03/5984 (downloaded 26 December 2015)

Smith, Philip & Max-Neef, Manfred (2011) *Economics Unmasked: From Power and Greed to Compassion and the Common Good*, Totnes: Green Books

Steffen, Will, Rockström, Johan, Cornell, Sarah, Fetzer, Ingo, Biggs, Oonsie, Folke, Carl & Reyers, Belinda (2015) 'Planetary Boundaries: Guiding human development on a changing planet' in *Science*, 347: 6223

Thomas, Sophie (2012) 'The Great Recovery' *RSA blog* [Online], www.thersa.org/fellowship/journal/archive... (downloaded 25 July 2013)

Trucost (2013) 'Natural Capital At Risk: The Top 100 Externalities of Business' London http://www.trucost.com/published-research/99/natural-capital-at-risk-the-top-100-externalities-of-business (downloaded 21 October 2015)

Watkins, Kevin (2013) 'Inequality as a Barrier to Human Development' in *Kapuscinski Development Lectures* Stockholm School of Economics http://kapuscinskilectures.eu/wp-content/uploads/2013/03/Kevin_Watkins_lecture.pdf (downloaded 14 August 2014)

Williams, Zoe (2015) 'Why Natalie Bennett should shrug off this 'humiliation" in *The Guardian*, London http://www.theguardian.com/commentisfree/2015/feb/24/natalie-bennett-shrug-off-humiliation-vision (downloaded 26 December 2015)

Towards a 'for everyone economy'?

KATHERINE TREBECK

Introduction

MANY OF US have become so busy we outsource almost everything – our cleaning, our care, our shopping. We outsource it to those who have little choice, but to take the poverty wages we flutter in their face. We pay others to pick boxes of cereal from the shelves of a massive supermarket – in part because, through our neglect, many local shops have closed down.

We do so wondering why we're stressed, wondering why inequality is rising within many countries, and wondering why people with jobs are queuing for food parcels.

It is because we let them.

We've let our economic system seemingly slip into the control of large companies. Over several decades we've let it become one that serves those with power and skills and 'cultural capital'; while those without these resources are expected to be grateful for the crumbs from the tables – miserly payments for laundering our shirts, washing our elderly relatives, driving the delivery vans full of the shopping we ordered online, mowing our lawns, and beyond our shores, sewing our trainers and sequined t-shirts so we can be 'on trend'.

The system behind this stems from a conception of economics that has misdirected too much of our politics and too many of our businesses – in Scotland, and in the UK. Our economy has become dysfunctional, seeking growth and profits, at – it seems – almost any cost and inadequately sharing the resources people need to build lives worth living.

In the natural world the concept of 'enough' – of sufficiency; of saturation – is well understood. Yet in the orthodox economics that ostensibly directs policy making at all levels of government, there seems to be little appreciation of limitations to growth as currently pursued. Instead the goal of more, and faster, dominates. This goal outweighs any concern for distribution, let alone quality, of growth.

While economic growth has undeniably delivered important outcomes,[1] indications are that our economic model is no longer delivering for many beyond the fortunate wealthy few. Should Scotland not look to appreciate and enjoy the results of growth to date, instead of rushing for more?

For those countries and people which have more than their fair share, should we not be harvesting and savouring the fruits of growth before they rot any further? Of course growth is important – there are many countries and many communities which desperately need 'more' (be it education, health care, good jobs and so on). But calls for these places to grow must pay heed to *quality* of growth – the wrong sort of growth can be divisive and may not 'trickle down' to those who need it most. It may harm the environment which is so important for economic and human wellbeing.

At a time when Scotland is moving on from two big referendum debates into exploring how to use existing and new policy levers at its disposal, going beyond false binaries is crucial. This means recognising that there have indeed been notable benefits of growth thus far, but acknowledging diminishing marginal benefits and the increasing harm from incessant pursuit of growth without regard to its quality or distribution.

Rather than dwelling on the consequences of poor quality and badly distributed growth for people and planet (of which many others have given a good account[2]), an attempt is made here to explore what an economy truly 'for everyone' might entail. This would be an economy that delivers social justice and protects and cherishes the environment. Examples of 'practice' will be considered – ranging from business models that offer greater equality and sustainability, new methods of manufacturing, pro-social ways of organising work and employment, appropriate measures of national and business success, and initiatives that retain money and control for local communities.

These will be presented neither as essentials, nor as definitive components of a blue-print, but as a glimpse that a 'for everyone' economy is not only possible, but that in small, and still rather isolated pockets, is already in existence. Scotland (and other localities) can learn from the examples offered: they present a way of looking beyond flimsy hope that wealth for the few will trickle down to the many. They are connected by the need to move from quantitative growth to *quality* of growth that benefits those who need it most, first and foremost. And they point to the nature of an economy that proactively, concertedly and deliberately serves people and planet.

But before discussing some of these contours of a new economic paradigm, the problem of our current state of affairs will be briefly described. Then the notion of a new economic paradigm is set out in abstract terms, before discussion turns to the concrete examples.

The problem: misalignment

The outcomes of our economic and political system are too often misaligned with what we as people and communities want and need, and with what our planet requires to survive. Examples of misalignment include:

- As a planet we have exceeded four of nine planetary boundaries mapped by the Stockholm Resilience Centre.[3]

- The gap between rich and poor (the best off 1 per cent of British people have accumulated as much wealth as the poorest 55 per cent put together).[4] Globally, over half of the world's wealth is now owned by just 1 per cent of the population, and seven out of ten people live in countries where economic inequality has increased in the last 30 years.[5]

- Inequality of wealth is paralleled in a polarising labour market: employment is growing in top jobs; declining in mid-level jobs; and gradually gaining in low-skilled, low service sector roles.[6]

- Over the last few decades the majority of workers have seen little real wage rise, while an increasing share of national income goes to profit, and to the pockets of a few at the top (see Boyd's chapter). Since the 1970s there has been a process of 'trickle up' as more gains go to rich, especially the very rich.[7]

- Such inequalities contribute to further misalignment: inequality weakens social cohesion and trust; erodes sense of community; undermines community involvement; produces more crime and violence; is associated with more severe sentencing; produces worse health, education and general wellbeing; and generates economic instability.[8]

- Unequal distribution of 'factors of health' gives rise to (growing) health inequalities.[9,10] As the *British Medical Journal* warned in 1996 'what matters in determining mortality and health in a society is less the overall wealth of that society, and more how evenly that wealth is distributed'.[11]

- In the UK, almost 12 million people are too poor to engage in common social activities considered necessary by the majority of the population.[12] Rising numbers are turning to food banks: Oxfam and Church Action on Poverty calculated that over 20 million meals were given to people in food poverty in 2013/14 by the three main food aid providers, a 54 per cent increase from the previous year.[13]

- And to paper over this multifaceted misalignment, many people have gone into debt (in 2012 one in five adults had to borrow money to pay for day to day expenses).[14] This meant consumption levels were maintained through borrowing – described by Roberto Unger and Tamara Lothian as a 'pseudo-democratisation of credit [which] replaced a real redistribution of wealth and income'.[15]

- This is related to another misalignment: our (inevitably hopeless) attempts to fulfil intrinsic needs with extrinsic activities like consumption, with increasingly disastrous impacts on the environment. People's anxiety about their status (which influences another profound emotion – shame) can lead to rivalry and competition in the form of pursuit of positional goods.[16]

It is clear that there are some serious problems with our society and economy. And so it is perhaps unsurprising that people see few paths open to them beyond working harder, buying more, speeding up the hedonic treadmill, stressing more and panicking more; with some eventually submitting to the politics of fear, angry protest, despair, or hopelessness.

Many explanations might be put forward as to how this state of affairs has developed. Some might point to the way in which economic activity has focused on short term rewards, especially amongst shareholder-owned businesses,[17] linked to the increasing dominance of finance.[18] A growing number of thinkers are saying that the money supply,[19] the role of banks in creating money and an overall 'financialisation of society'[20] is a key culprit in the growth fetish driving our economy down a dangerous road. Others might highlight how economic growth in many western economies in the second half of 20th century relied heavily on expansion of a market in mass consumption goods.[21] Some might criticise how economies like Britain's are characterised by business strategies reliant on low pay, low quality and/or price competitive services.[22] Linked to this are criticisms of pursuit of labour market flexibility which has seen the replacement of salaried staff with temporary, casual and out-sourced labour as core-periphery models of business proliferate.

There are many more explanations – and of course they often intertwine and reinforce each other (see the other chapters in this book). In Scotland we see that it is a multifaceted nest of all of these dynamics that underpins and perpetuates Scotland's inequalities, our insufficient sustainability, and the too-often short term partisan debates.

A people-friendly economy: in abstract

A new economic paradigm?

In 1998, almost 20 years ago, James Robertson reflected that the main argument between 'conventional politicians'... is about how economic recovery is to be achieved. They will continue to voice this basic set of assumptions... until others have articulated clearly and coherently a new set of assumptions to succeed it'. Antonio Gramsci many years before him highlighted that a crisis is a historical moment in which the old world order is collapsing and a new world must first be fought for in the face of resistances and contradictions.[23] And Gar Alperovitz most recently has suggested that we are in the 'prehistory of truly fundamental change beyond traditional corporate capitalism, beyond state socialism. So all this experimentation [in our communities]... could be laying the foundations of something for the long-term'.[24]

These three observations point to the need for a new vision – a way of challenging the systemic nature of the misalignment outlined above. They suggest that having *something* to challenge economic orthodoxy is part of the process of creating that challenge.

The examples set out below are not necessarily the most crucial tenets of a new economic paradigm. They are offered as a window, a hint, and perhaps a bit of inspiration that new priorities, new goals, new processes, new structures even are *possible* – as Alperovitz says, the 'pre-history' of change.

They are efforts and ideas connected by the need to go beyond (narrow, extractive, harmful) economic growth to 'good development' through which a community or a country or even a planet can prosper and flourish.

Notions of 'good development' for Scotland need to reflect lessons of self-determination theory: that autonomy, competence and relatedness are basic human needs.[25] Access to resources, control over one's life, agency and ability to exercise choice are important factors in self-determination and mental health: Scotland's economy needs to deliver these factors.[26] Research into why some First Nations communities in Canada have relatively high rates of suicide amongst young men and why other communities do not, supports the notion that autonomy, competence, relatedness and coherence are key. The research by Chandler *et al* found that those Aboriginal communities which have been able to rehabilitate cultures (promoting cultural 'continuity' and preservation of heritage) could cherish their past, while also shaping a collective future (via devolution of control from government to community) were able to 'insulate' their youth from the risk of suicide.[27] This concurs with Giddens' notion of ontological security which describes how being a full participant in society gives autonomy, stability, and sense of control over life.[28] Similarly, American-Israeli sociologist Aaron Antonovsky found that a 'sense of coherence' is an important mechanism to promote good health and build resilience.[29] Antonovsky suggests coherence depends on comprehensibility (the extent to which events in one's life can be understood and predicted); manageability (having necessary skills and resources to manage and control one's life); and meaningfulness.[30]

One of the (perhaps many) lessons for Scotland's economic future that can be drawn from these diverse sources is that a new economic paradigm needs to ensure that people are not simply at the beck and call of others. Instead people need to be able to influence their tasks, and exercise direction over their future. People also need to have bonds – with a community (perhaps of place, perhaps of interest) and with a cultural past. They further need to feel secure – in themselves and their status, in their income and employment and, of course, in terms of their safety. This is a far cry from the experiences of many in Scotland – those on zero hour contracts, turning to food banks or subject to benefit sanctions.

In turn, this suggests that 'good development' requires greater *equality* – so people are not entangled in deleterious status anxiety and competition. It requires *quality jobs* for everyone – jobs which are designed to ensure people have direction over their tasks, satisfaction in their work, and knowledge that their employment is secure and provides income sufficient to participate in society with dignity. It requires strong *social safety nets* – so people know they will be supported when they experience misfortune. And it requires *control* – so people really are at the apex of policy making, rather than at the mercy of forces beyond their control.

Life in the 'doughnut'

Environmental sustainability is inherent in such notions of 'good development', but the impact of current mistreatment of the planet is stark. In Scotland, we fail to stay within safe environmental limits. While carbon emissions have been moving in the right direction we still see recommended safe limits breached in Scotland by over 470 per cent, and in land-use change and nitrogen cycles we see breaches of over 250 per cent.[31] In terms of air quality, safe levels are being breached in 12 per cent of road testing sites, and over half of our fish stocks are being unsustainably harvested.

It now takes the planet one year and six months to replenish what humanity uses each year.[32] We have moved past the 'safe operating space' for four of the nine planetary boundaries (climate change, land use change, biodiversity loss and alteration of the nitrogen cycle).[33] This is perhaps most vividly evident in the increasing speed of melting snow and ice every year[34] or the 405 'dead zones'[35] proliferating in the ocean.[36] Each year, 315,000 people die from climate change induced weather and other impacts, with another 325 million seriously affected.[37] The poorest are always earliest hit and hardest hit. It is no wonder that Kenneth Boulding bemoaned that '[a]nyone who believes in infinite growth on a finite planet is either a madman or an economist'.[38]

To explore different ways of pursuing good development, Oxfam shared the concept of a 'safe and just' operating space for humanity that exists below the planetary boundaries, but above a social foundation of human deprivation.[39] This posits a profound repurposing for the economy – away from GDP growth towards meeting the needs of people and planet. This depends on quality and distribution of economic activity, rather than growth *per se*.

The plausibility of recasting economic growth in such a way is bolstered by the work of Peter Victor who modelled the Canadian economy under various growth scenarios for 30 years (2005–2035).[40] John Stuart Mill, many, many years before Victor, forecast a 'stationary state' which would follow a phase of growth when the economy would reach constant population and constant stock of capital; but with continued human development in the form of 'mental culture, and moral and social progress... [and] improving the Art of Living'.[41]

The next section casts a wide net for examples of policies and practices that have potential to contribute to improving Scotland's economy so it works for the vulnerable and/or eases pressure on the planet. Together, and with many others, they can move humanity into that *safe* and *just* operating space and better align the outcome of Scotland's economic activity with what people and planet need – in Scotland, the UK, and beyond.

A people-friendly economy: in practice

Realignment and redistribution

Realigning the economy and politics with what people and communities really want and need requires redistribution to better align opportunities for those at the bottom. Demographer Danny Dorling has warned that we cannot keep plastering over 'wounds caused by inequality by building more prisons, hiring more police and prescribing more drugs'.[42]

The socio-economic inequalities dividing the UK and Scotland are not inevitable: there was a relatively narrow gap between the richest and the poorest in the UK from 1945 to the late 1970s. And it is also possible to cite other countries with substantially less inequality than the UK. Inequality is a product of an economic model created by choices we have made over many years: the type of jobs on offer; their remuneration; who gets what work; the sectoral composition of the economy; and so on. What matters are the incentives we provide for businesses to behave in certain ways; the way and what we tax; the operation of the planning system; how much we support those experiencing hard times; and so on (many, though not all, of these are already the remit of the Scottish Government). For example, out of work benefits in the UK fall short (by 60 per cent) of a consensus based Minimum Income Standard for a single adult.[43] But, concurrently the UK is in the 'top league of countries to place increased pressure on benefit claimants'.[44] Another example: the National Minimum Wage is well below the rate of the minimum income standard,[45] while inequality *within* firms has risen in the UK.[46]

Taxation is an important lever to help shape the sort of society and economy we want:

- It can build in incentives so that managers take account of long term social and environmental goals[47]

- It can be used to tax unearned good fortune[48]

- It can redistribute by ensuring the whole tax system is robust and progressive[49]

Shifting the tax burden to capital, wealth and harmful activities should be intuitive, yet politicians (including Scottish politicians) often claim that doing so would lead to 'flight' of the 'wealth creators'. Leaving aside that 'trickle down economics' from such wealth creators has hardly eventuated, the reality is that the number of people who move for tax reasons is negligible, even amongst the wealthy – usually only a few celebrities.[50] For example, Jon Shure (Director of Fiscal Studies at the Centre on Budget and Policy Priorities) describes 'tax flight [as] a myth... no [US] state has ever raised taxes and lost money'.[51]

How we spend tax revenue is also a key factor in creating a more equal society. Many studies show that after a certain point national wealth does not necessarily deliver social improvement:[52] it depends on what money is spent on. Health and education promote equality – today's outcomes shape tomorrow's opportunities.

Making the economy circular and shared

If we are to truly transform and lighten our impact on the planet we need to transform how we manufacture products and dramatically alter how we use them. This is about a shift from a take-make-waste linear business model to 'lease the resource, make the product, recover the resource and then remake it'.[53] In other words, an economy that is circular and shared.

Circular economy

There is a growing impetus to manufacture so resources are used 'from cradle to cradle'. This 'circular economy' mimics nature: there is very little waste; instead resources are available for another use. Part of the imperative for businesses is resource constraints – Ian Cheshire (of B&Q) says 'we are now faced with the need for real reinvention of our high resource-impact business models... Business models assuming an implicit abundance of free resources cannot by definition be sustainable'.[54]

A leading proponent of a shift towards circular manufacturing, the Ellen MacArthur Foundation, has reported that the EU could save at least £220 billion a year if products were designed to enable resource recovery and eliminate waste.[55] For example, every mobile phone uses 40 different elements:[56] as the price of these elements rises, so will the financial imperative to recover them.

While Scotland was the first nation to sign up to the Ellen MacArthur Foundation Circular Economy 100 network, which has sought to advance a circular economy via the establishment of Zero Waste Scotland, required change needs a shift in how products are designed. It is suggested that approximately 80 per cent of a product's environmental impact is 'locked in' at design stage.[57] So there is a need to 'redesign products in a cradle to cradle context so we run the whole recycling loop, making our value-add from controlling the component materials in the product rather than a one-time fire and forget sale'.[58] It requires eradicating 'planned obsolescence' whereby products are designed to wear out and be disposed of and instead create durable and long lasting items – fewer items, but with more users. For that, producers need to be both compelled and supported.

Sharing economy

A growing number of initiatives are embracing the idea of a 'sharing' (or collaborative) economy – in which people and workplaces recognise that they require a *service*, not the machine that produces it. Hence people might lease (perhaps higher-quality) a machine for a period of time, rather than purchasing (perhaps lower quality) ones and replacing them.[59] A well-known entrepreneur in this space is carpet company Interface – they do not provide carpet, but a 'floor covering service'. This means they sell the *service* of keeping a space carpeted; when tiles wear out they are replaced, collected, broken down, and remanufactured. This is a process which dramatically reduces resource use – people are sharing (via rental) scarce physical resources. In some instances 'fractional ownership' will allow people to share use of an item with others over time; in other circumstances the shared ownership will be simultaneous. Short term car hire might be an example of the former (see the model developed by the likes of Zipcar or Car Club); a single washing machine accessible by every flat in a communal stairwell an example of the latter. Sometimes the arrangement will be money orientated (as in the case of cars or carpets); in other instances it will be more about community relations and borrowing (tool libraries or one lawn mower for a street, for example); and often a combination of the two.

Realising a sharing economy requires us to revalue what assets we exchange and why and how we exchange them – quite a challenge to an economy in which ownership (of more) is so prominent. And it requires a move away from one of the fundamental tenets of capitalism – that of private property. This is evident in the observation by Nick Folland (Head of Group Corporate Affairs Director: Net Positive for Kingfisher)[60] that people do not need to own everything they once previously thought they should own. He explains: 'we could sell them an entry level tile cutter, which will do the job, just about, then sit on their shelf for years. Or we could lend them a top-end one'.[61]

Some policy makers are also recognising the benefits offered by a sharing economy. While Scotland's cities are making spaces for car sharing initiatives, Seoul shows there is scope to do more. Seoul is positioning itself as a model city for sharing.[62] The goal underlying these efforts is to create jobs and increase incomes; to address environmental challenges (for example, reducing unnecessary consumption and waste); and recover trust between people.

New notions of business purpose

The fair trade movement has often pointed to the willingness of consumers in the rich world to pay more for a product if it could be demonstrated (via kite marks and so on) that the product is, *inter alia*, ethically sourced; environmentally sustainable in its manufacturing processes; or meets certain standards in labour use across the supply chain. But, a more pertinent question might be: why are consumers and societies prepared (or permitted?) to pay for something that is artificially cheap?

Currently, businesses externalise many costs – one corporation's actions and assets become liabilities for other parties, such as taxpayers, communities, and the ecosystem. This caused economist K William Kapp to suggest that

> capitalism must be regarded as an economy of unpaid costs, 'unpaid' insofar as a substantial portion of the actual costs of production remain unaccounted for in entrepreneurial outlays; instead they are shifted to, and ultimately born by, third persons or the community as a whole.[63]

The extent to which conventional business models insufficiently account for environmental cost is seen in recent analysis by Trucost – they reported that if the world's major industries properly integrated for their environmental impacts, not one of them would be profitable.[64] In 2015 the IMF released estimates that support to fossil fuel companies

– taking into account environmental damage that other actors need to attend to – is equivalent to $10 million a minute.[65]

Behind this transfer of cost is an interpretation of fiduciary duty (many would say mistakenly) as a duty on corporate managers to maximise shareholder return. Moreover, this 'return' is invariably interpreted as short term share price increases and dividend payments. Incentive structures within firms (such as remuneration and promotion benchmarks) orientated to short term outcomes can further still discourage managers from addressing long term issues, even those which might impinge on future profitability.

Such interpretation means that social and environmental externalities are both over- and under- delivered. Negative environmental impact is over-delivered because firms do not sufficiently account for the impact of their operations. Socio-economic benefits are under-delivered because firms are not set up in a way that sufficiently incorporates wider socio-economic considerations into their decision-making framework. Similarly, negative social impacts are over delivered while positive environmental impacts are under delivered. For example, treatment of labour rarely takes account of social needs. It is clear that unemployment is harmful to individuals involved: to their mental and physical health; to their families; to their communities; and to the economy (which incurs additional outlay in benefits, while forgoing taxation revenue). Yet most firms operate within a system which casts labour as a cost to be reduced (evident in the way employees are increasingly treated as 'just-in-time' inventory; and in the way productivity is interpreted). In contrast, firms need to be encouraged to embrace labour use.

Shifting the tax base has been mentioned above, another mechanism is greater attention to impact on non-financial results (with reporting and audits as a prelude for action). Steps are being taken in this direction – legislation such as the UK Companies Act 2006 stipulates wider duties of company directors, including having regard for and reporting on the company's impacts on communities and environment, with s172 requiring companies to take account of interests beyond their shareholders. Beyond the UK, at least 86 companies have agreed to draw up natural capital accounting rules and in 2011 Puma published the first ever attempt to measure, value and report environmental externalities in a major corporation in the entire supply chain.[66]

Of course reporting is a far cry from action, so above and beyond this, businesses need to be driven by a sense of purpose to enhance communities (and conserve the ecological systems) where they operate. For example, a 'pro-social' orientation would flow from changing the duties of executives so that they are compelled to improve the welfare of society and customers, not just shareholders. This means 're-purposing' businesses so they internalise costs currently seen as externalities and imbuing in private organisations a wider, more collectively orientated purpose (so they generate positive externalities). Doing so might require a re-write of company law to rank employees, customers and society alongside shareholders as beneficiaries of the corporation.[67] In the US, Benefit Corporations are a legal structure[68] which requires companies to consider all stakeholders – not just shareholders – when making decisions. In the UK Community Interest Companies offer a similar broadening of scope – dividends to shareholders cannot exceed 35 per cent of profit and there has to be a demonstrable community or wider public purpose (over 8,000 CICs have opened since the scheme started in 2004).

Inclusive decision making is another part of re-purposing. A start would be company boards that represent a range of constituencies.[69] This could rebalance power across stakeholder groups (spreading ownership, ensuring employee representation on pay committees, and so on). Beyond the board, employees and managers can be incentivised differently via long term determinants of reward and promotion. For example, at Unilever managers' compensation is linked to sustainability goals and, in an effort to reduce short term orientation, Unilever no longer issues quarterly forecasts.

Organisational pluralism – pro-social businesses

Broadening out the considerations made by firms, how they account for impact and the way in which they report is clearly part of the picture, but the shape, structure and governance of the firm is another. Theories of 'the firm' remind us that firms originated as a political response to economic problems related to coordination and organisation of economic activity.[70] But what has emerged since is a particular notion of 'shareholder value' (mentioned above) which sees firms as comparable to other economic objects – which can be owned, traded and profited from. This perspective implies that satisfying shareholder interests is the overriding goal of management.[71] Tellingly, Jack Welch, former CEO of General Electric (and the man reputed to have coined the term 'shareholder value' in 1981) has recently admitted that 'shareholder value is the dumbest idea in the world'.[72]

One mechanism to democratise workplaces and imbed social and community values into the operation of a business is via business models that democratise ownership. Worker cooperatives, for example, mean that workers are employing the capital, rather than visa-versa. Although not perfect,[73] employee and community cooperatives present a way to do business that is better aligned to the needs of people and planet, rather than simply profit.[74] Cooperatives measure success not by profit, but by the flow of benefits to members. Cooperatives place democracy at the heart of decision-making and often an asset lock is in place that protects surpluses (with employees receiving a dividend). Those working for employee-owned firms also generate positive externalities, in the form of happier, healthier employees and surrounding communities.[75] The ownership structure often means money and jobs are kept in communities, supporting local purchasing power.

To increase the proportion of such 'pro-social' business models in the Scottish economy, there is a need for tax and other incentives to encourage transfer of ownership to workers – taxation will also signal sought behaviours and educate relevant professionals.[76] Similarly, the lever of procurement can create incentives to develop cooperative business models. Other mechanisms can be found in legislation – in

France profit-sharing is a statutory obligation for all companies with more than 50 staff members. Governments should also intervene financially to support the cooperative sector.

Finally, the positive relationship between density of locally-owned firms and per capita income growth is worth cultivating. Small, locally owned firms bring local benefit via labour costs (payment of wages and other benefits to local residents); profits (which remain in the community in proportion to local ownership); procurement of local goods and services for input and resale and operations; and charitable giving to local causes.[77] The contribution of locally-owned firms can be more than four times that of non-resident owned firms.[78] There is scope to explore how Scotland's rates and licensing regime could be more conducive to local ownership.

Better work

Within all enterprises, the way work is managed and controlled; the type of work; the pay and conditions of work; and the relationship workers have with each other is an opportunity for greater alignment between the economy and what people want and need. Yet many countries operate from an economic model which has taken the 'low road'. This entails allowing – sometimes even incentivising – businesses to operate low-cost, low-value-added business strategies. The Joseph Rowntree Foundation recently observed that 'the UK has a higher number of low-paid, low-skilled jobs than most developed countries'.[79] There are fewer demeaning jobs and fewer low-paid workers in Japan, Norway, Germany, Denmark, Switzerland, Netherlands, and Canada.[80] UNICEF has found that in the UK children fare worse than in other developed countries because of extremes of pay: long working hours and parents consequently having less time and energy for their children.[81] The rise of self-employment and zero hour contracts reflects a deepening of the 'core and periphery' model of employment in which increasing numbers experience insecure work.[82]

Moreover, the number of UK employees who feel they have a great deal of influence over their work has declined.[83] This lack of autonomy leads to depression, powerlessness, and a sense of inadequacy.[84] This is 'real' stress – when there is an imbalance between demands and control and between effort and reward.[85] People with high demands on their output, but low control over their tasks have higher risk of heart disease.[86] So there is a clear misalignment between the jobs people need and the jobs most people are able to find.

In contrast, people who say their work is meaningful, or serves some social and communal good, report better psychological adjustment; greater wellbeing; place a higher value on work; have greater job satisfaction; work more unpaid hours; are less prone to turnover; and have a greater commitment to the organisation.[87] Steger *et al* suggest that meaningful work encompasses skill variety; opportunity to complete an entire task; the significance of the task in the eyes of others; engagement; challenge; intrinsic work orientation; good pay; and reputation.[88]

Ways to change this are in the hands of policy makers, communities, and firms themselves (see Boyd's chapter, for further discussion); for example, requiring companies to report the proportion of their workforce paid below certain thresholds. As discussed above, employees should be represented on remuneration boards and given more say – even ownership – via democratic models of business. Rights for workers – particularly those without power in the employment relationship – need to be protected (already the UK has one of least regulated labour markets in the OECD).[89] Abolishment of wages councils and trade union reforms are likely to have resulted in the rise in low pay in the UK – reinstating mechanisms to bolster the power of workers are needed.[90]

Sharing work

Currently, work is poorly distributed. Too many people work long hours, while too many people want more hours. But long working hours are associated with anxiety;[91] with women more adversely affected by working longer hours than men.[92] Involuntary unpaid overtime is high in the UK: the TUC estimates that five million workers give one day a week in free overtime.[93] In contrast, others are under-

and unemployed: which, as seen earlier, has profound impacts on individuals (indeed, the loss of wellbeing through unemployment exceeds the reduction in income).[94]

The deleterious impact of both over- and under- work suggests that better sharing the available work would help align the economy with the needs of people and planet (it goes without saying that better sharing of work must deliver increased income to the poorest, via increased hourly pay and via increased hours for those currently under or unemployed).

The evidence shows that working less (out of choice) is associated with higher wellbeing than full time working.[95] The Netherlands provides a model for better sharing work: here, working less is the norm; one third of men work part time or compressed hours and it has low overall working hours (1377 hours a year compared to the American 1778 hours a year and the UK's 1647 a year).[96] Employees in the Netherlands have the right to request reduced working and the right to take career breaks of up to three years under the 'Life Course Savings Scheme'. Other mechanisms to reduce work time include a shorter working week; early retirement; increased holiday time; more part time working; job sharing; career breaks; and parental leave.

Shorter working weeks, for example, can have environmental benefits too: congestion will be reduced and carbon emissions will fall (so long as people do not replace work time with high material impact leisure activities, and instead adopt lower resource use activities).[97] Rosnick (2013) found that reducing work hours over the rest of the century by 0.5 per cent per year would eliminate a quarter to a half of global warming.[98]

With each other, for each other

Sharing work better is an opportunity to recover people's time for themselves and for each other – it means they can fortify social networks.[99] This not a frivolous concern: research from 2006 found that 9 million adults reported experiencing loneliness at weekends.[100] Others feel excluded by poverty: 22 per cent of adults – ten million people – felt embarrassed by their low income.[101] When people are deprived of feeling valued and connected to others as equals they are at risk of becoming mentally ill – our brains have developed so that most people cannot cope when they are not treated as equals, and psychosis is 'normal behaviour' when people live in social isolation.[102] Yet, as Schor warns, '[e]conomic growth undermined the need for community interdependence. When people can afford to purchase goods, they ask for favours less often… Prosperity itself can corrode community, by undermining our need for one another'.[103] This suggests that people have become alienated from each other.

Communities – of place and of interest – are mechanisms to bring people back together. The potency of community connections was highlighted by Sen who observed that in the 20th century periods in which life expectancy grew the most were those decades in which countries were at war – not those with the fastest economic growth.[104] He attributes this to the population bonding together. The creation of institutions such as the welfare state and the NHS in the UK emerged from the terrible hardship and fear of the Second World War – a time when people put aside class differences for the 'imagined community' of the nation.

People obtain greater wellbeing from giving to others compared to when they receive 'stuff'.[105] Creating a culture for kindness is necessary. This means promoting equality (discussed above) and empathy, rather than competition. Despite the structural, educational and cultural pressures in the opposite direction, humans are social animals, with the capacity to be empathetic and compassionate.

More time away from the work place is one way; free and safe community spaces another. A third is decentralisation to lower (and perhaps less formal) levels of government which might also help foster this sense of community.[106] For example, the process of Participatory Budgeting (pioneered in the Brazilian city of Porto Alegre in 1989 involving 20 per cent of the city's annual budget) is a bottom up process through which community members collectively decide how their local taxes are spent. In Scotland such mechanisms have been found to contribute to more robust self-governance, transparency, better-informed citizens, and more equitable access to decision-making and spending.[107, 108]

Decoupling aspiration from consumption

Human impact on the planet is skewed, with the richest people putting stress on the planet, and often the poorest suffering the consequences. For example:

- Global environmental decline can be attributed to less than 30 per cent of the world's population[109]

- Picketty and Chancel found that the top ten per cent of global emitters contribute about 45 per cent of all emissions, in contrast to just 13 per cent of emissions from the bottom 50 per cent of emitters[110]

- 12 per cent of people use 85 per cent of world's water[111]

- Five planets would be required if everyone in the world lived as people in the US do[112]

Such statistics are behind what environmentalist Herman Daly identifies as an 'impossibility theorem' – the notion that the world can attain US levels of per capita production and consumption.[113]

Thus, a new economic paradigm that keeps us all in a safe and just space requires we face up to disproportionate use of the earth's resources by some and the barriers this presents to lifting everyone above a social foundation. If there is to be room on this finite planet for the poorest communities to raise their standards of living, those consuming too much of the planet's scarce resources need to consider Gandhi's wish that people would 'live simply, so that others might simply live'.

This means that richer people 'decouple aspiration from consumption' and decouple remaining consumption from impact on the planet. The challenge is great given the manner in which our current economic model depends on people buying more and more products. As Victor Lebow (in)famously wrote in 1955 in the *Journal of Retailing*:

> our... economy demands that we make consumption our way of life... The measure of social status, of social acceptance, of prestige, is now to be found in our consumptive patterns... We need things consumed, burned up, worn out, replaced, and discarded at an ever increasing pace[114]

Veblen noted many years ago that in modern urban societies, when people do not know each other, their wealth (and imputed status) is advertised by conspicuous consumption. In wealthy countries and for wealthy consumers anywhere, products are less about basic needs, but (as Veblen wished) they have taken on a role as symbolic communicators: conveying social status, constructing identity, differentiating from or joining others.[115]

Inequality further undermines people's need for esteem. The more anxious people are about their status, the more consumption is seen as a means to assert a sought position in the socio-economic hierarchy.[116] The very real human need to belong to and be esteemed by one's peer group is exploited by marketers in ways that encourage consumption. Greater equality is thus important in breaking the loops between status anxiety and consumption.

But even in more equal societies – and particularly in less equal ones – other levers need to be pulled. For example, we need businesses to stop advertising in a way that turns wants into needs. This might include limiting the tax-deductibility of advertising or banning excessive advertising (following the example of Quebec which, in 1980, banned advertising aimed at children).[117] A more challenging step forward would be to make greedy behaviour socially unacceptable, while embracing the value, satisfaction and fun derived from *experiences* as opposed to the acquisition of things (already many older people spend less of their income on things and more on experiences which have a lower material impact).[118]

In reducing the impact of what we do consume, improvement in the quality of what is consumed is a step forward.[119] The shift towards a circular economy in which there is more sharing, rather than direct ownership of items (as discussed above) is a useful mechanism to realise this shift.

New measures of prosperity: knowing when we're aligned

There is no shortage of research, writing and evidence highlighting the deficiency of Gross Domestic Product as a measure of economic, let alone societal, progress. GDP merely measures (albeit rather poorly) economic activity – money changing hands. It was designed by Simon Kuznets who warned that 'the welfare of a nation can scarcely be inferred from a measurement of national income as defined [by GDP]'. Any relationship between economic growth and job creation (so called Okun's law) is relatively weak and varies between countries – in the past, in the US a 3 per cent increase in GDP led to a one per cent fall in unemployment; in France, a 3 per cent increase in GDP led to a 0.5 per cent fall in unemployment; and in Japan there is no such relationship.[120] Trickle down is not a given (and, as seen earlier, it has been more a case of 'extract upwards').

GDP has failed to signal when human productive activities become 'uneconomic' – when the incremental benefits are overwhelmed by costs.[121] Pursuit of GDP without equivalent or greater regard for other indicators of real progress is no longer improving people's lives in wealthy nations and is putting more and more pressure on the planet.

The need for better and multiple measures of progress is not in doubt: there will be different measures for different uses. But across these, taking account of people's views, needs and preferences is important. Exclusively expert or elite authored measures are another form of elite capture, inequality and democratic deficit. Measurement cannot be seen as a value-neutral activity: Stiglitz, Sen and Fitoussi (2009) argue for tools based on societal discussion of aims and desires, so that people collectively decide what they want their society to be.[122] As Khalid Malik, author of the UN's Human Development Report notes: 'only the wearer may know where the shoe pinches, but pinch-avoiding arrangements cannot be effectively undertaken without giving voice to the people and giving them extensive opportunities for public discussion'.[123] Sen, in the *Idea of Justice* (2009) similarly emphasises the role of public discussion and deliberation in constructing more just institutional arrangements and states of affairs.

In creating measures of what a new economic paradigm needs to achieve, the selection of measures, policies and priorities thus needs to be done democratically, involving all components of society. This bestows legitimacy for chosen indicators and ensures the measure is trusted by citizens and recognised as shared knowledge.[124] For example, in Scotland, Oxfam has developed a measure of the country's progress that seeks to put people at the apex of policy making. Rather than simply adopting the views of think tanks, academics or other 'experts', and rather than using arbitrary weightings for respective components, the composition of Oxfam's Humankind Index is a direct reflection of the views and priorities of the people of Scotland.[125]

Conclusion – growth of the new?

The ideas and changes suggested above are merely a selection of those necessary to move Scotland into the safe and just space of a new economic paradigm. Much is missing – for example, the role of the money supply; how global trade might operate; the crucial importance of the core economy; the rights of future generations; and much more.

These, and the examples offered here, do speak to a wider, ambitious notion of development in which Scotland's 'progress' is understood not as increases in GDP, but 'improvement in the sustainable and equitable wellbeing of a society' – via material living standards; health; education; environment; political voice and governance; security; employment; social cohesion and, perhaps most importantly, greater equality. The UNHDR defines human development as the multidimensional conception of possibilities people have for leading a good life. The economic and political changes discussed in this paper are part of reclaiming this wider, expansive understanding of development from all-too narrow confines as economic growth, wealth creation, and consumption.

The practices and changes briefly outlined in this chapter demonstrate that a new economic paradigm requires Scotland to collectively embrace the notion of 'enough' – enough stuff, enough consumption, and enough income for everyone. But, to be really transformative we need to go beyond worthwhile activities to address underlying structures of Scotland's economy. This will require long term planning and budgeting[126] and real preventative spending, not just sticking plasters. In this, at its core, a new economic paradigm is about justice rather than charity, it is about repurposing the economy according to, as we have already discussed, the needs of both people and planet.

Notes

1   Look no further than the halving of people living in extreme poverty has been halved (down to 22 per cent in 2010); five years ahead of the United Nation's MDG target (Deen, 2013). There is also the steady, long term advances for most, but not all, nations and groups in educational and health status over the last few decades (Walton, 2010: 1)

2   See, for example, Watkins, 2013; Childs and McLaren, 2012; Magdoff and Bellamy Foster, 2011; Branko Milanovic cited in Staff Reporter, 2011 2013; Resolution Foundation, 2012; and Dorling, 2010.

3   http://www.stockholmresilience.org/21/research/research-programmes/planetary-boundaries.html

4   Inman, 2014

5   Credit Suisse, 2015

6   Resolution Foundation, 2012: 11

7   Lansley, 2006: 23

8   Wilkinson and Pickett, 2009

9   Marmot, 2004: 14

10   Aldridge *et al.*, 2012

11   Quoted in Stuart, 2011: 12

12   Gordon *et al.*, 2013

13   Cooper *et al.*, 2014

14   Gordon *et al.*, 2013

15 Lothian and Unger, 2012

16 Schor, 2011: 177; Jackson, 2009

17 Childs and McLaren, 2012: 20

18 Davies, 2009: 26. The UK economy is now more reliant on financial services than the USA, France, Germany or Japan, yet as recently as 1992 it was least dependent on finance of those nations.

19 See, for example, http://www.positivemoney.org/

20 Gongloff, 2012

21 Lothian and Unger, 2012

22 Pennycook and Whittaker, 2012: 39

23 Cited in Beck, 2013

24 Alperovitz, 2013

25 Deci and Ryan, 2008

26 The process behind this is extreme inequality making people feel more anxiety about status and threats to their self-esteem – and this anxiety causes the stress hormone cortisol to be released, increasing blood sugar and suppressing the immune system. (Marmot, 2004: 14). Additional counter-productive strategies can include comfort eating, violence and abuse of alcohol.

27 Chandler *et al.*, 2003. The researchers found sustaining a workable sense of personal persistence, self-continuity, acceptable grounds for imagining themselves as continuous in time led to decreased adolescence suicide; providing 'identity preserving connections' which keep young men from moments of despair and give them a reason to care for their future.

28 Sociologist Anthony Giddens (cited in Marmot, 2004: 205) has described 'ontological security' as the confidence that most human beings have in the continuity of their self-identity and the constancy of their social and material environments. It requires a sense of the reliability of persons and things; having trust in the world; being confident in the social order, their place in society, their right to be themselves and a belief that self-realisation can be achieved.

29 Walsh *et al.*, 2013: 42

30 Cited in (Walsh et al., 2013: 42). Antonosky was drawing on studies of women who survived Nazi camps and developed the concept of salutogenesis – focusing on factors which promote health and wellbeing and the relationship between health, stress and coping.

31 Sayers and Trebeck, 2014

32 United Nations, 2012: 47

33 SRC ref

34 At the end of summer Arctic sea ice in 2007 was 40 per cent down in size than in late 1970s when measures began, and the last three years with the least Arctic sea ice cover at end of summer were 2007, 2008, and 2010 (Magdoff and Bellamy Foster, 2011: 13).

35 Due to chemical run off and surface warming.

36 Figure as of 2006, compared to the 49 dead zones recorded in the 1960s.

37 Schor, 2011: 15

38 United States. Congress. House (1973) Energy reorganization act of 1973: Hearings, Ninety-third Congress, first session, on H.R. 11510. p. 248

39 Raworth, 2012

40 These were business as usual; a no growth disaster (in which greenhouse gasses level off); or stable economic growth via planned and deliberate change and policy interventions such as those outlined in the following section. The latter scenario requires new meanings and measures of progress, limits on material and energy consumption, waste production and conversation of natural lands; stable population and labour force; more efficient capital stock; more durable/repairable products; better pricing, inc carbon price; shorter work years/more leisure time; reduced inequality; fewer status goods; more informative/less deceptive advertising; better screening of technology; more local trade; education for life (cited in (Dietz and O'Neill, 2013: 50,51))

41 JS Mill *Principles of Political Economy with Some of their Application to Social Philosophy* quoted in (Dietz and O'Neill, 2013: 203)

42 Dorling, 2010: 318

43 Harkness, 2012: 36

44 Daguerre and Etherington 2009 quoted in Harkness, 2012: 15.

45 Davis *et al.*, 2014: 34

46 Davies, 2009: 32

47 For example, more tax levied on these companies with extreme earnings inequality or undertaking polluting activities; a lower rate for those activities which are sustainable and contribute to social goals.

48 Such as an inheritance or a windfall gain.

49 Including taxing wealth, the value of land, and capital more heavily than labour.

50 Stewart, 2013

51 Quoted in Stewart, 2013

52 See, for example, http://www.socialprogressimperative.org/data/spi.

53 Thomas, 2012

54 Cheshire, 2011

55 See http://www.forumforthefuture.org/greenfutures/articles/great-
recovery-closing-gap-between-materials-and-design

56 Such as copper, indium, gold – by some measures there is more gold in a
tonne of mobile phones than in a tonne of mined rock from a gold mine (and
it is easier to extract gold from a phone than from a mine) (Thomas, 2012).

57 Thomas, 2012

58 Cheshire, 2011

59 Thomas, 2012

60 Owner of UK hardware company B&Q which is exploring ways to
integrate sharing economy principles into its operations.

61 Cited in Wright, 2013

62 For example, it is expanding sharing infrastructure; promoting sharing
enterprises; incubating sharing start ups via provision of office space,
consultation services and subsidies; creating a Sharing Promotion
Committee; subsidising the expenses of ten sharing enterprises; vetting
and designating sharing enterprises; providing access to data and digital
works; correcting obstructive statutes; opening government parking lots
and municipal buildings to the public during idle times; connecting senior
citizens with extra rooms to students; and creating tool libraries and
shared bookshelves in communities (Johnson, 2013).

63 Quoted in Magdoff and Bellamy Foster, 2011: 40

64 Trucost cited in (Roberts, 2013). The majority of unpriced natural capital
costs are from green house gas emissions (38 per cent); water use (25 per
cent); land use (24 per cent); air pollution (7 per cent); land and water
pollution (5 per cent) and waste (1 per cent).

65 Coady et al, 2015

66 Environmental information was converted into data that had monetary
terms, revealing that in 2010 72 per cent of Puma's profits would
disappear if the company had to pay for environmental impact. PPR
– Puma's parent company – has since committed to creating
environmental profit and loss accounts for all its luxury brands (including
Gucci and Yves Saint Laurent).

67 Hargraves, 2013

68 In 2010 Maryland became the US first state to pass a Benefit Corporation
bill (now 19 other states have followed).

69 Hargraves, 2013

70 Cited in Davies, 2009: 40

71 Davies, 2009: 13

72 Cited in Guerrera, Francesco, 'Welch denounces corporate excesses', *Financial Times*, 13 March, 2009.

73 Challenges of producer organisations include: they may require members to own land; cultural barriers to participation of women; they might discriminate against vulnerable people with fewer assets; problems of free-riders and dishonest members; the risk of being captured by local elites (Sahan and Fischer-Mackey, 2011)

74 Davies, 2009: 25

75 Davies, 2009: 93. See also Erdall, 2011

76 Davies, 2009: 95

77 Rodriguez and Houston, 2007

78 Fleming and Goetz, 2011. See also Patel and Martin, 2011.

79 Schmuecker, 2014

80 Dorling, 2010: 160

81 Cited in My Fair London, 2012: 16

82 Trebeck, 2011

83 Felstead 2007 cited in Davies, 2009: 54

84 Bauman in Hanlon and Carlisle, no date

85 Marmot, 2004: 122

86 As evidenced in The Marmot 'Whitehall study' (which engaged with 10,000 civil servants) showed that stress increases as descended the organisational hierarchy, and this is linked to greater levels of heart disease; see (Marmot, 2004).

87 Steger *et al.*, 2012

88 Steger et al., 2012

89 Silim, 2013: 11

90 Pennycook and Whittaker, 2012: 14

91 Abdullah and Shah, 2012 3

92 Abdullah and Shah, 2012 23

93 Trades Union Congress, 2012

94 Abdullah and Shah, 2012 17

95 Abdullah and Shah, 2012 3

96 Dietz and O'Neill, 2013: 135

97 Schor, 2011: 114

98 Rosnick, 2013

99 Schor, 2011: 7

100 Cited in Dorling, 2010: 266

101 Gordon *et al.*, 2013

102 Dorling, 2010: 271

103 Schor, 2011: 140–141

104 Cited in Marmot, 2004: 169

105 For example, the richest are best able to turn money into happiness if they give it away (New Scientist, July 2012)

106 Of course, one does not want to romanticise such processes – their benign success is dependent on local social and political context; there is potential that transfer of power locally might simply reinforce existing inequalities and practices.

107 Harkins and Egan, 2012

108 It is heartening to see the Scottish Government encourage local authorities to deploy 1 per cent of their budget via Participatory Budgeting.

109 Nariinder Kakar, Permanent Observer to the UN of the International Union for Conservation of Nature in (United Nations, 2012: 52)

110 Chancel and Piketty, 2015

111 United Nations, 2012: 52

112 In 2006 the average American emitted 19.7 metric tons of CO_2, compared to the 10 tonnes on average per head in Germany, Japan, and Britain; Italy's 8.3 tonnes; France's 6.7 tonnes; Ch 4.6 and India 1.3 tons ((Schor, 2011: 44))

113 Quoted in Magdoff and Bellamy Foster, 2011: 32

114 Quoted in Magdoff and Bellamy Foster, 2011: 49

115 Schor, 2011: 27

116 See, for example, Schor, 1999

117 See sections 248 and 249 in the Quebec Consumer Protection Act: http://www2.publicationsduquebec.gouv.qc.ca/dynamicSearch/telecharge.php?type=2&file=/P_40_1/P40_1_A.html

118 Dietz and O'Neill, 2013: 160

119 Rosnick, 2013

120 Dietz and O'Neill, 2013

121 Smith and Max Neef, 2011

122 Stiglitz *et al.*, 2009

123 Malik, 2013

124 Hall and Rickard, 2013: 24

125 See www.oxfam.org.uk/humankindindex: Oxfam asked almost 3,000 of them what they needed to live well in their communities (focusing on collective assets), making a particular effort to reach out to seldom-heard communities and creating time and space for deliberation, discussion and debate. This generated a set of priorities which were

weighted to reflect the relative importance of each factor of prosperity
relative to the others.

126 For example, Oregon's ten year budget process.

References

Abdullah, Saamah and Shah, Sagar (2012) *Wellbeing patterns uncovered: an analysis of* UK *data* new economics foundation: London: http://www.neweconomics.org/blog/entry/well-being-patterns-uncovered-a-new-wealth-of-data-for-the-uk (downloaded 22 July 2014)

Aldridge, Hannah, Kenway, Peter, MacInnes, Tom and Parekh, Anushree (2012) *Monitoring Poverty and Social Exclusion* 2012 Joseph Rowntree Foundation: York.

Alperovitz, Gar (2013) *What Then Must We Do? Straight Talk About the Next American Revolution*, Green Press Initiative: White River Junction.

Arterian Chang, Susan (2010) Moving towards a steady-state economy. *The Finance Professionals' Post.*
//post.nyssa.org/nyssa-news... (downloaded 13 August 2012)

Beck, Ulrich (2013) 'Why 'class' is too soft a category to capture the explosiveness of social inequality at the beginning of the twenty-first century'. *The British Journal of Sociology*, 46: 1, 63–74.

Chancel, Lucas and Piketty, Thomas (2015) 'Carbon and inequality: from Kyoto to Paris Trends in the global inequality of carbon emissions (1998–2013) and prospects for an equitable adaptation fund' Paris School of Economics: Paris
http://piketty.pse.ens.fr/files/ChancelPiketty2015.pdf (downloaded 9 December 2015)

Chandler, Michael, Lalonde, Christopher & Sokol, Hallett (2003) *Personal Persistence, identity Development, and Suicide: A Study of Native and Non-Native North American Adolescents* Vancouver: http://web.uvic.ca/~lalonde/manuscripts/2003-Monograph.pdf (downloaded 19 October 2012)

Cheshire, Ian. (2011) 'Imagining a New, Sustainable Capitalism'. *The Guardian*, 24 March 2011.
http://www.theguardian.com/sustainable-business/blog/kingfisher-ceo-ian-cheshire-sustainable-capitalism (downloaded 21 May 2013)

Childs, Mike and McLaren, Duncan (2012) *Mapping a Route from a Planet in Peril to a World of Well-being* Friends of the Earth: London.

Coady, David, Parry, Ian, Sears, Louis & Shang, Baoping (2015) 'How Large Are Global Energy Subsidies?'. International Monetary Fund (ed.) *Working Paper*. 15/105: Washington http://www.imf.org/external/pubs/cat/longres.aspx?sk=42940.0 (downloaded 2 March 2016)

Cooper, Niall, Purcell, Sarah and Jackson, Ruth. (2014) *Below the Breadline: The relentless rise of food poverty in Britain* [Online]. Oxford. http://policy-practice.oxfam.org.uk/publications/below-the-breadline-the-relentless-rise-of-food-poverty-in-britain-317730 (downloaded 15 July 2014)

Credit Suisse (2015) 'Global Wealth Report 2015' Zurich https://publications.credit-suisse.com/tasks/render/file/?fileID=F2425415-DCA7-80B8-EAD989AF9341D47E (downloaded 9 December 2015)

Davies, William (2009) *Reinventing the Firm* Demos: London: www.demos.co.uk/publications/reinventing-the-firm (downloaded 23 December 2009)

Davis, Abigail, Hirsch, Donald and Padley, Matt (2014) *A Minimum Incomes Standard for the UK in 2014* Joseph Rowntree Foundation: York: http://www.jrf.org.uk/sites/files/jrf/Minimum-income-standards-2014-FULL.pdf (downloaded 15 July 2014)

Deci, Edward & Ryan, Richard (2008) 'Self-Determination Theory: A Macrotheory of Human Motivation, Development, and Health' in *Canadian Psychology*, 49: 3, 182–185

Deen, Thalif. (2013) 'Poverty Declines and Inequality Deepens'. *Inter Press Service*, September 2013. www.ipsnews.net/2013/09/poverty-declines-as-inequality-deepens/ (downloaded 1 October 2013)

Dietz, Rob and O'Neill, Dan (2013) *Enough is Enough: Building a Sustainable Economy in a World of Finite Resources*, Routledge: Abingdon.

Dorling, Danny (2010) *Injustice: Why Social Inequality Persists*, Bristol: The Policy Press.

Erdall, David (2011) *Beyond the Corporation – Humanity Working*, London, The Bodley Head.

Fleming, A and Goetz, S. J (2011) 'Does Local Firm Ownership Matter?'. *Economic Development Quarterly*, 25: 3.

Fuentes-Nieva, Ricardo & Galasso, Nicholas (2014) *Working for the Few: Political capture and economic inequality* Oxfam International: Oxford: http://www.oxfam.org/en/policy/working-for-the-few-economic-inequality (downloaded 15 July 2014)

Gongloff, Mark. (2012) 'Michael J. Sandel Warns Market Society Risks America's Soul'. *The Huffington Post*, 13 April 2012. http://www.huffingtonpost.com/2012/04/13/michael-j-sandel-market-society_n_1424733.html (downloaded 15 July 2014)

Gordon, David, Mack, Joana, Lansley, Stewart & et al (2013) *The Impoverishment of the UK: PSE UK First Results – Living Standards* ESRC: http://www.poverty.ac.uk/sites/default/files/attachments/The_ Impoverishment_of_the_UK_PSE_UK_first_results_summary_report_ March_28.pdf (downloaded 22 July 2014)

Hall, Jon and Rickard, Louise (2013) People, Progress and Participation: How Initiatives Measuring Social Progress Yield Benefits Beyond Better Metrics. In Bertelsmann Stiftung (ed.). Berlin: http://www.bertelsmann-stiftung.de/cps/rde/xbcr/SID-ECFCC74B-C1DB6044/bst/xcms_bst_dms_37947_37948_2.pdf (downloaded 22 July 2014)

Hanlon, Phil and Carlisle, Sandra (no date) *Reflections from Scotland, Consumerism: Dissatisfaction Guaranteed* Afternow: Glasgow: http://www.afternow.co.uk/papers/6-consumerism-dissatisfaction-guaranteed/89-reflections-from-scotland (downloaded 12 October 2012)

Hargraves, Deborah. (2013) 'Does the Shareholder Owned Company Have a Future?'. *High Pay Centre* [Online], http://highpaycentre.org/blog/does-the-shareholder-owned-company-have-a-future (downloaded 22 July 2014).

Harkins, Chris and Egan, James (2012) *The Role of Participatory Budgeting (PB) in Promoting Localism and Mobilising Community Assets: But Where Next for PB in Scotland? Learning from the Govanhill Equally Well Test-site* Glasgow Centre for Population Health: Glasgow: http://www.gcph.co.uk/latest/news/322_participatory_budgeting_ learning_from_govanhill_equally_well_test_site (downloaded 22 May 2013)

Harkness, Susan, Gregg, Paul and MacMillan, Lindsey (2012) *Poverty: The Role of Institutions, Behaviours and Culture* Joseph Rowntree Foundation: York: http://www.jrf.org.uk/sites/files/jrf/poverty-culture-behaviour-full.pdf (downloaded 19 October 2012)

Inman, Phillip (2014) 'Britain's richest 1% own as much as poorest 55% of population' in *The Guardian*, 15 May 2014, London http://www.theguardian.com/uk-news/2014/may/15/britains-richest-1-percent-own-same-as-bottom-55-population (downloaded 2 March 2016)

Jackson, Tim (2009) *Prosperity Without Growth? The Transition to a Sustainable Economy* Sustainable Development Commission: London: http://www.sd-commission.org.uk/publications.php?id=914 (downloaded 8 July 2010)

Johnson, Cat. (2013) 'Is Seoul the Next Great Sharing City?'. *Shareable* [Online], www.shareable.net/blog/is-seoul-the-next-great-sharing-city (downloaded 24 July 2013).

Kuznets, Simon (Acting Secretary of Commerce) 1934. National Income, 1929–1932: Letter from the Transmitting in Response to Senate Resolution No. 220 (72nd Cong.). 73rd US Congress, 2d session, Senate document no. 124, page 5–7.

Lansley, Stewart (2006) *Rich Britain: The Rise and Rise of the New Super-Wealthy*, Politico's Publishing: London.

Lothian, Tamara and Unger, Roberto (2012) Stimulus, Slump, Superstition and Recovery: Thinking and Acting Beyond Vulgar Keynesianism. *Juncture*. ippr: London: www.ippr.org/juncture/171/9818/stimulus-slump-superstition-and-recovery... (downloaded 3 June 2013)

Magdoff, Fred and Bellamy Foster, John (2011) *What Every Environmentalist Needs to Know About Capitalism – A Citizen's Guide to Capitalism and the Environment*, New York.

Malik, Khalid (2013) *Human Development Report 2013: The Rise of the South* United Nations Development Programme: New York: http://hdr.undp.org/en/2013-report (downloaded 22 July 2014)

Marmot, Michael (2004) *The Status Syndrome – How Social Standing Affects Our Health and Longevity*, Holt Paperbacks: New York.

My Fair London (2012) *Why Inequality Matters* Centre for Labour and Social Studies: London: http://classonline.org.uk/pubs/item/why-inequality-matters (downloaded 11 October 2012)

Patel, Amar and Martin, Garrett (2011) *Going Local: Quantifying the Economic Impacts of Buying from Locally Owned Businesses in Portland* Policy, Maine Centre for Economic: Maine.

Pennycook, Matthew and Whittaker, Matthew (2012) *Low Pay Britain* Resolution Foundation: London: http://www.resolutionfoundation.org/publications/low-pay-britain-2012/ (downloaded 22 July 2014)

Raworth, Kate (2012) *A Safe and Just Space for Humanity – Can We Live Within the Doughnut?* Oxfam: Oxford GB http://policy-practice.oxfam.org.uk/publications/a-safe-and-just-space-for-humanity-can-we-live-within-the-doughnut-210490 (downloaded 29 November 2012)

Resolution Foundation (2012) *Gaining from Growth: the Final Report of the Commission on Living Standards* London: http://www.resolutionfoundation.org/media/media/downloads/Gaining_from_growth_-_The_final_report_of_the_Commission_on_Living_Standards.pdf (downloaded 22 July 2014)

Roberts, David. (2013) 'World's Top Industries Shown to be Unprofitable...'. *Green Economy Coalition* [Online], //greeneconomycoalition.org/know-how/world... (downloaded 14 June 2013).

Rodriguez, Heather and Houston, Dan (2007) *Procurement Matters: The Economic Impact of Local Suppliers* Civic Economics: Austin: http://bealocalist.org/sites/default/files/file/Local%20First%20studies/procurement-matters.pdf (downloaded 22 July 2014)

Rosnick, David (2013) *Reduced Work Hours as a Means of Slowing Climate Change* Center for Economic and Policy Research: Washington: http://www.cepr.net/documents/publications/climate-change-workshare-2013-02.pdf (downloaded 22 July 2014)

Sahan, Erinch & Fischer-Mackey, Julia (2011) *Making Markets Empower the Poor* Oxfam GB: Oxford: http://policy-practice.oxfam.org.uk/publications/making-markets-empower-the-poor-programme-perspectives-on-using-markets-to-empo-188950 (downloaded 14 August 2014)

Sayers, Malcolm and Trebeck, Katherine (2014) 'The Scottish Doughnut: A Safe and Just Space for Scotland' in Oxfam GB, Oxford http://policy-practice.oxfam.org.uk/blog/2014/07/the-scottish-doughnut-a-safe-and-just-operating-space-for-scotland (downloaded 2 March 2016)

Schmuecker, Katie (2014) *Future of the UK Labour Market* Joseph Rowntree Foundation: York: http://www.jrf.org.uk/sites/files/jrf/poverty-jobs-worklessness-summary.pdf (downloaded 11 July 2014)

Schor, Juliet (1999) The New Politics of Consumption. *Boston Review*. Boston: http://bostonreview.net/BR24.3/schor.html (downloaded October 2012)

Schor, Juliet (2011) *True Wealth: How and Why Millions of Americans are Creating a Time-Rich, Ecologically Light, Small-Scale, High Satisfaction Economy*, Penguin: New York.

Silim, Amna (2013) *Job Creation: Lessons from Abroad* Trades Union Congress: London

Smith, Philip and Max-Neef, Manfred (2011) *Economics Unmasked: From Power and Greed to Compassion and the Common Good*, Green Books: Totnes.

Staff Reporter. (2011) 'Global Inequality: Tackling the Elite 1% Problem'. *The Guardian*, May 2011. www.guardian.co.uk/global-development/poverty-matters/2011/nov/28/... (downloaded 21 May 2013)

Steffen, Will, Rockström, Johan, Cornell, Sarah, Fetzer, Ingo, Biggs, Oonsie, Folke, Carl, Reyers, Belinda 2015. Planetary Boundaries: Guiding human development on a changing planet. *Science*, 347: 6223

Steger, Marti, Dik, Bryan and Duffy, Ryan (2012) 'Measuring Meaningful Work: The Work and Meaning Inventory'. *Journal of Career Assessment*, 00: 0, 1–16.

Stewart, James. (2013) 'The Myth of the Rich Who Flee From Taxes'. *New York Times*, 15 February 2013. www.nytimes.com/2013/02/16/business/high-taxes-are-not-a-prime-reason-for-relocation... Downloaded 5 May 2013

Stiglitz, Joseph, Sen, Amartya and Fitoussi, Jean-Paul (2009) *Report by the Commission on the Measurement of Economic Performance and Social Progress* Commission on the Measurement of Economic Performance and Social Progress: Paris:

www.stiglitz-sen-fitoussi.fr/documents/rapport_anglais.pdf (downloaded 7 October 2009)

Stuart, Elizabeth (2011) Making Growth Inclusive – Some Lessons from Countries and the Literature. Oxford: Oxfam International

Thomas, Sophie. (2012) 'The Great Recovery'. *RSA blog* [Online], www.thersa.org/fellowship/journal/archive… (downloaded 25 July 2013).

Trades Union Congress (2012) Total Unpaid Overtime Worked is Equivalent to a Million Extra Jobs. London: http://www.tuc.org.uk/workplace/tuc-20446-f0.cfm (downloaded 2 February 2012)

Trebeck, Katherine (2011) *Whose Economy? The Winners and Losers in the New Scottish Economy* Oxfam: Oxford: http://policy-practice.oxfam.org.uk/publications/whose-economy-winners-and-losers-in-the-new-scottish-economy-118965 (downloaded 29 August 2011)

United Nations (2012) *Defining a New Economic Paradigm: The Report of the High Level Meeting on Wellbeing and Happiness* New York: http://www.uncsd2012.org/content/documents/519BhutanReport_WEB_F.pdf (downloaded 19 October 2012)

Walsh, David, McCartney, Gerry, McCullough, Sarah, van der Pol, Marjon, Buchanan, Duncan & Jones, Russell (2013) *Exploring Potential Reasons for Glasgow's 'Excess' Mortality: Results of a Three-City Survey of Glasgow, Liverpool and Manchester* Glasgow Centre for Population Health, NHS Health Scotland and University of Aberdeen: Glasgow: http://www.gcph.co.uk/assets/0000/3828/Three-city_survey_report_2013.pdf (downloaded 22 July 2014)

Walton, Michael (2010) *Capitalism, the State, and the Underlying Drivers of Human Development* UNDP: New York:

Watkins, Kevin (2013) Inequality as a Barrier to Human Development. In Stockholm School of Economics (ed.) *Kapuscinski Development Lectures*. http://kapuscinskilectures.eu/wp-content/uploads/2013/03/Kevin_Watkins_lecture.pdf (downloaded 14 August 2014)

Wilkinson, Richard and Pickett, Kate (2009) *The Spirit Level – Why More Equal Societies Almost Always Do Better*, Allen Lane: London.

Wright, Martin. (2013) 'Kingfisher's plan to put 'net positive' into practice'. *The Guardian*, 31 May 2013. www.guardian.co.uk/sustainable-business-kingfisher-plan-net-positive-practice downloaded 10 June 2013

Do we really want a more equal Scotland?

STEPHEN BOYD

This essay aims to describe the origins of rising income inequality and point the way towards some solutions. In doing so it seeks to highlight problems with the prevailing political economy of Scotland.

Introduction

ALL OF A sudden it seems everyone is worried about the consequences of rising inequality. Politicians across a remarkably wide spectrum, civic organisations, NGOs, media commentators and academics struggle to find space in an increasingly frenzied policy discourse. Even the global economic institutions – the IMF, World Bank and OECD – hitherto gleefully aggressive designers and implementers of the Washington Consensus, are publishing extensively on the roots and effects of inequality within and between nations. The tide of economists and policy entrepreneurs offering analysis and solutions rises ever higher. It's astonishing to recall that inequality studies was a niche pursuit as recently as a decade ago.

The issue of rising inequality was raised relentlessly during the referendum on Scottish independence. In keeping with the general tenor of the campaign, factoids, tropes and plain error crowded out reason and sober analysis. Did anything resembling a coherent plan to reduce inequality emerge from the froth? Of course it didn't. Indeed, many factors contributing to rising inequality continue to be completely ignored, some might say deliberately so. After all, if inequality is to be reduced, some fundamental power asymmetries will have to be confronted; a pursuit unlikely to attract many senior Scottish politicians.

There may have been no shortage of political wind on the subject, but beyond the excellent, increasingly important work of Stirling University economists[1] and a few illuminating Brian Ashcroft blogs,[2] there has been scandalously little serious work completed on inequality in Scotland. The consequence is that the trajectory and drivers are inadequately understood and many factors that surely exert a heavy influence remain obscure and apparently politically untouchable.

What follows is a run through some issues which require to be addressed if economic inequality in Scotland is ever to fall. In each section I try to explain how certain factors are likely to have influenced inequality, the ways in which the response in Scotland has been inadequate and provide some thoughts on how positive change might be nurtured. It's an unavoidably incomplete list. But first:

Precision

> Refusing to deal with numbers rarely serves the interests of the least well-off.
>
> THOMAS PIKETTY[3]

It's probably too much to ask that contributors to the debate on inequality in Scotland could be precise about the nature of the problem they perceive, the evidential base from which they draw and the solutions they propose. It would be rather wonderful if they could steer away from the factoids and lazy half-truths which currently pepper their arguments, even if such fluff does make for effective web flyers.

For a start it would be good to know if contributors are referring to the UK or Scotland. Scotland is certainly not the *fourth most unequal country in the world.* Is it inequality of income or wealth? Is it inequality of market incomes or income post tax and transfers? Has the measure been adjusted to take account of in-kind benefits (which across OECD nations reduce inequality by around one-fifth on average) from public services?

The popular narrative is that income inequality in the UK and Scotland has followed an upwards linear trend since the 1980s and that no serious policy interventions have been attempted. But as with so much popular economic discourse in Scotland the narrative dissolves under the slightest scrutiny. The upwards trend – steep and steady in the 1980s but much slower and more volatile since – has been far from linear. Some policy interventions have significantly and enduringly – if ultimately insufficiently – reduced income inequality.[4]

Trying to identify effective remedies is all the more difficult when false narratives on the extent and trajectory of inequality in Scotland and the UK are replayed on a daily basis. The UK is too unequal. Inequality is a massive problem. Climate change apart it's probably the biggest we face. It has profound social, political and economic consequences. But as some of us kept saying about the public finances back in 2010; there is no problem so great it can't be exaggerated or distorted. And that, I'm afraid, is what's currently happening.

Inequality is different from poverty

In the last decade – predating the 2008 economic crises – the incomes of those in the middle have come under pressure. But that squeezing of the middle has not happened because there has been greatly increased redistribution to the poor. Rather, what has happened is that shares of all other income groups have been squeezed as the share of the very top has soared, bolstered by the ability of those finding themselves able to extract what economists call 'rents' from the particular positions they are in, and by the rising importance of returns to wealth. It is the rich who have got more expensive, not, as has been alleged, that the 'cost' of the poor has risen.[5]

JOHN HILLS

It often seems Scottish politicians struggle to distinguish between inequality and poverty. For the policy solutions offered (eg childcare) could have a significant impact on the lives of people at the lower end of the household income distribution without achieving a great deal in reducing overall income inequality. An effective inequality reduction strategy must surely attack the problem from both ends.

The fact is that neither of our two main, ostensibly social democratic parties has proposed anything of substance to constrain income growth at the very top. For clarity, a slightly higher marginal top rate of income tax set at a very high threshold really doesn't begin to cut it. Strategists know that any serious attempt to address runaway executive pay – when adjusted for size of firm the UK has the highest executive pay in the world – will provoke strong pushback from well-funded interests. Why bother when poverty reduction is such safe territory, especially when the UK Government is targeting through austerity the benefits and services on which the poor depend?

It's difficult to take politicians fretting about inequality seriously when the policy response remains so transparently ineffective. It is of course a good thing that the poorest and most vulnerable people in society should be a priority for policymakers. But the problem of rising inequality in Scotland, the UK or the rest of the world cannot and will not be solved by ignoring those factors that have caused inequality to increase.

What is distinct about the UK?

On all credible measures the UK is a highly unequal society. But regularly proclaiming that the UK is the 'fourth most unequal country in the OECD' is ultimately a pointless pursuit if similar energy isn't applied to investigating how it became so and designing appropriate remedial policy strategies. It's remarkable therefore that during the referendum campaign not one single serious report was forthcoming that aimed at identifying the unique factors that have led to relatively high UK inequality and how independence might lead to different outcomes.

Contrary to the popular view of the Scottish Left, the UK is a reasonably redistributive society. The problem is that market inequality in the UK is exceptionally high. But why is it so? Any solution must lie in a forensic analysis of what is distinct about the UK system – why it produces such inequality in market incomes. Maybe the answer lies in the UK's industrial structure and business culture? Or the scale and political clout of the finance sector and the Anglo-Saxon shareholder model that seems uniquely adept at funnelling income upwards? The salient point is that, beyond rhetoric about Reindustrialising Scotland[6] (offering policy solutions that could largely be delivered under pre-Smith devolution), the Scottish Government has been silent on these issues.

It should also be remembered that Scotland, lacking the tier of super-earners located mainly around London and the South-East, is significantly more equal than the UK as a whole; mid-range for income inequality amongst OECD nations. It is reasonable to surmise that a strategy to reduce income inequality in Scotland might look somewhat different to a strategy for the UK as a whole.

The drivers

> ... the fact that high-income countries with similar technological and productivity developments have gone through different patterns of income inequality at the very top supports the view that institutional and policy differences play a key role in these transformations. Purely technological stories based solely on the supply and demand of skills can hardly explain such diverging patterns. What is more, within countries, we have to explain not only why top shares rose but also why they fell for a sustained period of time earlier in the twentieth century...[7]
>
> ALVAREDO, ATKINSON, PIKETTY AND SAEZ

At least part of the reason why politicians have often appeared so reluctant to grapple seriously with income inequality is the assumption that there's little domestic policy can achieve. Rising inequality is, so we are told, the inevitable consequence of *skill biased technological change* (SBTC) and trade – global trends over which national governments can exert little if any influence. An increasingly hour glass shaped labour market is the inescapable result. Why waste scarce resources trying to develop mechanisms to mitigate that which is beyond our control?

The extent to which global trends have influenced the level of inequality is in fact a highly contentious matter. For instance, Galbraith's seminal study[8] (2012) found that SBTC and trade were of little consequence. After all, these are genuinely global trends yet hugely different trajectories in inequality have been observed between within and between nations.

Recent research has focused more on the role of norms (Eg acceptance of high executive pay and rewards) and institutions (Eg diminishing role of collective bargaining) and is proving more successful in explaining the differences observed between, and changes over time within, nations. This work also better explains the prodigious success of the top one per cent in accumulating an ever rising share of total income. It also shows that domestic policy can, should and must have a role in addressing income inequality.

Given this intellectual shift, why has the orthodoxy on rising inequality been so rarely challenged? The first and most obvious reason – and one that suggests it's reasonable to cut Scottish politicians at least some slack – is that the dynamics of rising inequality were under-researched and poorly understood until relatively recently leaving a vacuum that orthodox theory was only too ready to fill.

But while that might explain the belated curiosity of policymakers, it's hardly a convincing excuse for the failure to adopt coherent approaches by the time of the independence referendum, especially given the impetus provided by the great financial crisis. There are other less sympathetic explanations.

As noted in the introduction, taking a serious norms and institutions approach to tackling inequality immediately forces policymakers to directly confront entrenched economic power. There are few examples of such confrontation in recent times. Rather, with excuses huddling under the umbrella of 'competitiveness', what business has asked for, it has tended to receive. Businesses and their highest paid workers are lightly regulated and inadequately taxed.

Buying into the 'it's the inevitable consequences of SBTC and globalisation' hypothesis does however meet political imperatives: it confers an air of sophistication and hard-nosed realism. It says 'I understand global economic trends and I'm prepared to confront them head on'. But actually it's all too easy a response; one guaranteed a sympathetic hearing in the media and swathes of academia. Challenging orthodoxy requires confidence on the subject matter and the passion and bravery to find workable solutions.

As Krugman[9] has pointed out, the SBTC/trade hypothesis has a superficial plausibility that politicians and economists find attractive: the timing seems to work, it's just supply and demand and therefore obviously not the fault of Government. The longer these shibboleths remain unchallenged, the more deeply embedded becomes the orthodoxy. The ever diminishing capacity of the Scottish media and Parliament's growing inability/willingness to scrutinise means that challenge is often absent.

Tax

> ... the most obvious policy difference – between countries and over time – regards taxation[10]
>
> ALVAREDO, ATKINSON, PIKETTY AND SAEZ

If any one aspect of policy shines a light on the poverty of Scotland's political economy it is tax, an issue on which the political class happily advertises its hopelessness. Nothing demonstrates the analytical shortcomings and imagination deficit of what passes for a Scottish think tank community more than when they feel compelled to spout forth on tax. Academia seems largely uninterested. Too many 'Civic society' organisations earnestly criticise welfare reform whilst determinedly avoiding the difficult stuff around tax, pretending instead that the better society can be constructed simply by tackling avoidance and evasion.

A consequence of the original devolution settlement leaving the respective tax responsibilities of the Scottish and Westminster Parliaments highly unbalanced, tax hasn't played the central role in Scottish democratic discourse that it does in most mature democracies. Anyone expecting the referendum campaign to compel participants to take tax more seriously would've been sorely disappointed.

The SNP and Scottish Government insisted that tax would not rise in an independent Scotland; desperately clinging to the fantasy that the White Paper's proposals could be delivered on current levels of tax thereby precipitating Scotland's transformation to a Nordic society. Conveniently ignoring the propensity of public spending to rise with GDP, a think tank, ostensibly of the left, chipped in to assert – risibly – that all that was required was the creation of more and better jobs.

The timid and regressive Council Tax freeze continued to be posited as part of the bold 'social wage', the Scottish Government's bulwark against Westminster austerity. The freeze, which benefits most those in the higher bands and shifts more of the burden of funding essential services onto fees and charges, must surely stand as a testament to the timorousness of post-devolution Scottish Government.

Meanwhile, having finally managed to identify it as a weakness, Labour played remorselessly on the SNP's pre-2015 obsession with corporation tax cuts as an economic 'lever' (the economic lever – a metaphor careful chosen to imply a mechanical relationship between economic policy and outcome which is of course wholly false). But Labour's credibility on business taxation was hardly boosted by its silly, partisan opposition to the supermarket tax on the grounds of competitiveness. One might reasonably conclude that its approach to tax is cynically tactical.

Not a single voice on the left of the Yes campaign managed to summon the intellectual honesty to admit that the Nordic society they desire and promote so relentlessly simply cannot and will not be funded on current levels of taxation. Disgracefully, some continue to punt the line that higher levels of tax will flow from the more and better jobs that will be created post independence – a plan that (if it works at all – economic development in an advanced economy like Scotland is a tortuously difficult, uncertain and long term process) will lead inevitably to tax falling as a percentage of GDP unless rates are increased or new taxes implemented; the opposite of what needs to happen.

For my money, any future Scottish Government with a genuine

commitment to addressing inequalities of income and wealth must – over time – endeavour to make progress in at least four areas:

Increase tax revenues as a proportion of GDP: the international evidence[11] is clear – in tackling inequality it is the quantity of tax collected, not the progressivity of specific tax schedules that matters most in tackling inequality. And those countries that consistently achieve significantly higher total tax revenues do so with systems more regressive than Scotland's: everyone has to pay more, usually through higher labour taxes and significantly higher consumption taxes. This tax take is then used to fund the transfers that reduce inequality. At some point people will have to accept that it is probably impossible to design and implement a highly progressive tax system (of course income tax should be progressive but the system will not be funded sustainably simply by taxing the rich and corporations more) that will prove durable in a globalised world.

As US commentator Steve Randy Waldman has argued:

> We should recognize that, as a political matter, there may be tradeoffs between the scale of benefits and progressivity of the taxation that helps support them. We should be willing to trade some progressivity for a larger scale. Reducing inequality requires a large transfers footprint more than it requires steeply increasing tax rates. But, ceteris paribus, increasing tax rates do help. Also, high marginal tax rates may have indirect effects, especially on corporate behavior, that are socially valuable. We should be willing sometimes to trade tax progressivity for scale. But we should drive a hard bargain.[12]

And to clarify: *I'm not arguing this will be easy.* Increasing tax revenues as a share of GDP in a way that is fair and sustainable will be tremendously difficult. Scotland's tight integration with UK wide labour and product markets is likely to prove a major impediment to radical tax policies. But please cease with the Nordic rhetoric if you're not prepared to give it a try.

Raise the top rate of income tax: it's worth noting that all the Nordic nations have a higher top rate and that these rates kick in at a much lower threshold than the UK's lower top rate. This is significant not because it reflects the progressivity of their *systems* – it doesn't – but rather that it points to a recognition that, as Waldman argues above, high marginal tax rates may have positive indirect effects. There is no correlation between cuts in the top tax rate and economic growth but there is a very strong correlation between cuts in the top tax rate and rising pre-tax income: the UK and US have over the past forty years implemented some of the largest cuts in the top rate of tax yet experienced comparatively moderate growth. Both have however witnessed some of the largest increases in pre-tax incomes of the top one per cent.[13]

This suggests that *the response of pre-tax top incomes to top tax rates is due to increased bargaining power or more individualised pay at the top than increased productive effort.*[14] Lower top tax rates encouraged top executives to switch efforts back to securing a larger share of the profits. These increases in Remuneration therefore came at the expense of retained profits, investment, employment and wages for the ordinary worker. Lower top tax rates have therefore stimulated not patient long term investment but rent extraction and short-termism. Burgeoning remuneration for the top one per cent is bad for income and wealth inequality, bad for democracy and bad for jobs and investment.

Sustain a fair level of Inheritance tax: is there a more effective bellwether of a political party/movement's commitment to tackling inequality? Yet I can't recall a single mention of Inheritance tax in the referendum debate. If Piketty is correct that the rate of return on capital will outstrip the growth rate through the 21st century then an effective Inheritance tax set at a fair rate (and in this instance there should be no hesitation in stating that fair equals high) is essential. It's a depressing sign of the times that so few are prepared to make the case; a case that should be as obvious as it is overwhelming. Choose not to have a fair Inheritance tax; deserve to have society run by the rentier class. It's as simple as that.

Of course the Scottish Government doesn't (yet) possess this particular power. Yet it has rarely been shy about discussing issues over which it currently exerts little of no control; witness its enduring focus on Corporation Tax. This is an emblematic issue and one on which we should know where the Scottish Government and opposition parties stand.

Localise: the data suggests that those nations which collect more tax at a local level, consistently manage to collect more tax in total. Scotland and the UK are heavily centralised in this respect, collecting roughly 95 per cent of tax centrally, but the majority of European states – especially the Nordics – collect much more locally (in 2012 Denmark collected 27 per cent of total tax revenues locally and Sweden 35 per cent). Building on the work of the Commission for Strengthening Local Democracy, it is necessary to devolve tax powers within Scotland. It would be helpful if the opportunity was taken to turn business rates into a system of land value tax. The Council Tax can be genuinely and quickly reformed while options for its replacement are reconsidered. This would involve as a minimum new bands, higher multipliers and regular revaluations. A viable replacement for the Council Tax must retain property at its core. The opportunities to design new taxes to suit specific circumstances must be provided to local authorities. Experience elsewhere suggests smaller, more accountable democratic units will develop the trust necessary to develop and maintain a sufficient and durable local tax base.

Financialisation and inequality

The study of national experiences substantially confirms the evidence of the global statistics. In rich countries such as the US, we find that economic performance has become dominated since 1980 by the credit cycle; financial booms and busts drive the performance of employment and thus prosperity is associated with rising income inequality. Further, as we examine the structure of rising inequality we find practically everywhere the same signature of a rising share of total income passing through the financial sector. The difference between the financial sector and other sources of income is – wherever we can isolate it – a large (and even the prime) source of changing inequalities. In the wake of the crisis, as we observe directly in the US and Latin America, the financial sector shrinks and inequalities tend to moderate[15]

JAMES K. GALBRAITH

Consider this – in the UK between 1979 and 2007:

- The top decile (ten per cent) increased their share of total income by 14 percentage points, from 28.4 per cent to 42.6 per cent.

- The top percentile (one per cent) accounted for fully two-thirds of these gains, seeing their share rise from 5.9 per cent to 15.4 per cent.

- 60 per cent of the increase in income share accruing to the top percentile has gone to financial service employees although they account for only around one-fifth of such workers.[16]

Is there anyone left out there who really believes that these outcomes were fair reward for talent and effort expended in a perfectly competitive labour market? That in less than 20 years, a few senior bank executives increased their productivity to the extent they were worth an additional 6 per cent of total income? Maybe there's something about the structure of the industry that needs addressing? Maybe too big to fail, too large to manage, too powerful to incarcerate institutions were looting their customers and wider economy? In Scotland's cowardly political economy, these issues are anathema.

Growing the financial sector *as an end in itself* has been a consistent priority of *all administrations* since devolution. Even the financial crisis and great recession/stagnation that followed haven't caused the Scottish Government to fundamentally reassess the role of finance in the Scottish economy. The argument is stuck in a horribly familiar groove: Scotland has a comparative advantage in banking and financial services (especially asset management) which should be built upon using Scotland's cost advantage over London to attract more activity – whether it is 'challenger' retail banks or higher value activities like investment banks. There are no trade-offs and the distributional consequences – in as much as they're considered at all – are assumed to be benign.

But the evidence tells us something very different.[17] Financialisation is bad for the economy and worse for society. It contributes to rising inequality in a number of ways beyond simply enriching its participants: a greater share of total national wealth shifts to the financial sector; the financial sector functions in a way that is detrimental to the productive economy (it refuses to fund patient company growth or higher risk innovative activity) and by forcing firms to focus on immediate shareholder value.

There has been hardly a squeak from any of Scotland's mainstream parties about financialisation's negatives. The White Paper was silent on this as it was on so many of the factors that would have to change if Scotland is to become a more equal nation. None of the inquiries launched by Government or Parliamentary Committees post crisis have comprehensively assessed whether or not growing the financial sector is, in and of itself, a positive economic benefit to the nation. There has been no reversal of the prioritisation of financial voices in policy debate; despite all that has happened financial services are still assumed to be the repository of the best brains in the country. After all, their pay must signal something?

A more enlightened approach would be to cease gibberish about rebalancing the economy through growing manufacturing. The size, power and biases of finance prevent the nurturing of manufacturing through patient investment in people, plant and research. Structural and regulatory reform of finance is a prerequisite for a fairer, more stable economy and stronger democracy. It is a sad reflection on Scotland's political economy that no mainstream party has felt confident post 2008 in taking such a straightforward approach to reform.

Corporate Governance

The UK model of corporate governance has distributional consequences. Power resides in the hands of one set of stakeholders, and they are, compared with their peers in most other developed nations, very short term in outlook. The consequence is 'a high distribution of profits to this cohort at the expense of ploughing back these profits (as increased investment) or distributing them to workers as higher wages'.[18]

Poor corporate governance is also manifested in the ethically bankrupt system of executive remuneration where directorships are shared amongst a tight coterie who happily sit on each other's remuneration Committees in a transparently 'you scratch my back...' system. The incentives created by lowering the top rate of income tax do not necessarily lead to higher pay and perks for the top one per cent. They only do so because they're facilitated by weak corporate governance.

This issue more than any other highlights the crossover between rising inequality and industrial short-termism. But despite the political class rediscovering the joys of 'making things' just as it started getting interested in inequality, the linkages – and what these reveal about the UK's economic and social model – remain obscure.

Incredibly while the Scottish Government relentlessly attacked the failures of the UK model and its performance vis-à-vis other nations; a mature consideration of the factors that make the UK model what it is – and would have to change if Scotland is to develop differently – was wholly absent. For instance, the don't frighten the horses approach exemplified in the call for formal currency union would have left the structure and regulation of finance as a UK responsibility; corporate governance never rated a single mention; no reforms were suggested that would help extend investment horizons; no mention of company law and beyond a welcome call for better gender balance, nothing that would change the composition of boards. Astonishingly, the independence White Paper had nothing whatsoever to say about ownership. It is as if the mere mention of these issues might be sufficient to provoke capital flight. Project Timidity?

Confronting asymmetries of bargaining power... or how we moved from the Treaty of Detroit to Washington Consensus

Many economists attribute the average worker's declining bargaining power to skill-biased technical change: technology augmented by globalization heavily favors better educated workers. In this explanation, the broad distribution of productivity gains during the Golden Age is often assumed to be a free-market outcome that can be restored by creating a more educated workforce. We argue instead that the Golden Age relied on market outcomes strongly moderated by institutional factors. Following the literature on economic growth that emphasizes the role of institutions in economic outcomes, we argue that institutions and norms affect the distribution of economic rewards as well as their aggregate size[19]

LEVY AND TEMIN

Inequality ultimately reflects the relative bargaining power of different economic agents. Asymmetries of bargaining power become even more acute when there is a structural deficit in decent employment. Those at the bottom struggle by on minimum wage, zero hour contracts while those at the top can effectively set their own remuneration. The Nordic nations have managed to sustain the highest levels of trade union membership and collective bargaining coverage and they are currently the most equal nations in the world.

While the relationship between inequality, trade union density and collective bargaining coverage is now widely discussed in papers by the IMF and articles in the FT, it's hardly at the forefront of political debate in Scotland and the UK. Yes, the White Paper makes some encouraging noises which were quickly followed up in the Working Together review; a document setting out a very different vision of industrial relations to that being promoted by the UK Coalition Government. The Scottish Government's markedly different approach is now being developed through the Fair Work Convention. This represents genuine progress.

Yet doubt must persist over whether the Scottish Government

really understands the nature and extent of the challenge. Its talk of European style *social partnership* fails to acknowledge the huge differences in culture and institutions that render such a system so difficult to achieve in the Scottish context. The atomised Scottish employer lobby can hardly be compared to the employer pillars that help support social partnership arrangements around Europe. Scottish employer representative bodies have very low density, no analytical resources between them and at least some are nakedly ideological in outlook. The Federation of Small Business (who do at least make an effort) aside, their collective input into the policy process borders on laughable.

Union density and collective bargaining coverage have declined in most advanced nations; the Nordics stand out in sustaining relatively high levels (although the trajectory is slowly downwards here too). This reflects not only the impact of hostile public policy but also structural shifts in employment that are unlikely ever to be reversed. Therefore, again, some caution should be applied when considering what's achievable in any constitutional scenario: if Scotland wants (and, yes, that's a big 'if') to achieve Nordic rates of union density/collective bargaining coverage then it will by definition by a long term and difficult project.

Government played a role in reducing trade union influence and so it might not be too unreasonable to suggest that it might play a direct role in rebalancing power in the workplace. Access to social security entitlements is conditional on trade union membership in some nations; Nordic rates haven't just happened by accident.

The regulated wage floor

One of the damaging consequences of the assumption that inequality has risen on a linear trend is that positive policy impacts have been obscured if not completely ignored. There should be little doubt that introduction of the National Minimum Wage and tax credits around the turn of the century made a significant difference in the UK.

Recognising that too many workers currently don't benefit from collective bargaining, boosting living wage coverage must also remain a priority. Given that the Procurement Reform Bill has now been passed, it is necessary to agree the content of the strongest possible Statutory Guidance and effectively promote it to public bodies undertaking procurement. The action taken by a number of key private sector firms, particularly SSE in pushing the Living Wages through the supply chain provides a detailed model which can be promoted to other larger companies.

However, given that the increase in inequality over the longer term has been driven more by runaway wage increases at the top end of the distribution rather than stagnating wages at the bottom, we should be careful not to claim too much for the impact of increasing the minimum wage or wider introduction of the living wage. The NMW has become the standard in too many sectors and efforts to widen use of the Living Wage will need to be undertaken in conjunction with changes to benefits to ensure household incomes rise across the lower half of the distribution.

Economic Development

One positive feature of the early years of devolution was the vigorous debate over the best way to use Scotland's new and extensive powers over economic development. By the time of the referendum debate it seemed to have become an issue of little interest. While much energy was expended on an awful, deceitful debate over macroeconomic powers, economic development was relegated to a non-issue. But it's one that will have to be addressed if Scotland's economy is to develop in way conducive to a fairer distribution of income.

Approaches to address inequality based on the creation of 'more and better' jobs lack credibility. Whilst a more effective economic development strategy that does result in a higher employment rate and higher wages is undoubtedly desirable, the outcomes of any such strategy are necessarily long term and highly uncertain.

It will be necessary to supplement the current key sector led approach with a foundational[20] economic strategy for Scotland which concentrates on labour absorbing, sheltered economic sectors like supermarkets and other retail, utilities, transport, retail banking and the public sector where most people actually work. The social franchises which underpin economic activity in these areas should be utilised to boost job numbers and quality. Democratisation and localisation of the institutions and processes of economic development will also help communities derive better economic outcomes from development.[21]

Ownership, control and outsourcing

Privatisation has contributed to rising inequality in a number of ways: solid revenue streams previously available for public reinvestment become economic rents for the few; stable secure lower skill/wage jobs become insecure minimum wage jobs; decisions reflect the interests of shareholders abroad rather than the democratic will of domestic citizens and the quality of inequality reducing services diminished. Further privatisation and outsourcing will inevitably tend to reduce the pool of decent jobs and increase inequality.

These issues just aren't discussed in Scotland where discussions about ownership and control have become incredibly narrow and constrained. The defence of the NHS is the most blatant case, rarely addressing the reasons for higher health inflation or the best and worst features of other health regimes around the world.

Beyond health and education, it is generally assumed that, in the globalised economy, ownership and control must be left only to the market. The fact that there are distributional consequences is overlooked or ignored. Astonishingly, ownership never became an issue during the referendum campaign despite foreign ownership of key industrial sectors like whisky and oil having social as well as economic consequences. The UK's intensely relaxed approach to ownership isn't shared by any other European nation or, for that matter, the United States. It is yet another peculiar characteristic of the UK model on which the Scottish Government appears reluctant to comment let alone act.

Macroeconomic policy

Macroeconomic policy has distributional consequences but these tend only to be discussed with reference to fiscal policy: austerity is widely recognised to be a regressive policy but the distributional impact of monetary policy is often neglected. The jury may still out on the distributional consequences of quantitative easing (which boosted asset prices and therefore the wealth for those at the top but also very likely helped stabilise the economy and employment) but a narrow and inflexible inflation targeting regime is in the longer term probably incompatible with a stronger, fairer and more broadly based Scottish economy.

Conclusion

As a policy rule, this analysis suggests that reduction of inequality is generally and at best a slow affair. It is the consequence, in general, of steady institutional progress over a long period of time. Dramatic reductions in inequality are rare, and they may not be especially desirable. Politically driven increases in inequality on the other hand are often quite sudden; at any given moment, they may just be a coup, a civil war, or a collapse in regime type away[22]

JAMES K GALBRAITH

It was no surprise that Tony Atkinson's *Inequality: what can be done?* featured heavily in the economic pundits' lists of books of 2015 (FT, the Economist etc). Professor Atkinson is probably the world's leading researcher of inequalities of income and wealth and is a teacher of and latterly co-author, with Thomas Piketty, of 2014s publishing sensation *Capital in the 21st Century*. Atkinson has published pioneering work on inequality since the 1960s but this is his first major book aimed at a general audience.

Inequality is a very different book to *Capital*. Piketty's tome is a monumental work of scholarship from which a new theory of capital and inequality is derived. Atkinson's purpose may be less grand but is likely to prove of more practical use to policymakers: 'to set out concrete policy proposals that could... bring about a genuine shift in the distribution of income towards less inequality'.

His policy proposals form a very rare thing: a coherent and ambitious programme to reduce inequality. Some of his proposals are open to reasonable challenge on grounds of intent or practicality. The salient point is however that a programme of this scale and ambition is required to reduce what are now deeply embedded inequalities of income and wealth. By all means take issue with the detail, but any ostensibly social democratic politician making a virtue of their concern over inequality should be prepared to match Atkinson's broad vision.

On assuming the role of First Minister, Nicola Sturgeon emphasised the priority she placed on tackling inequality. It's appropriate therefore to compare the programme proposed by the world's leading inequality researcher to the policies actually being delivered at Scottish level. True, some of Atkinson's proposals are set firmly in reserved territory. Some straddle the devolution settlement. Others could be implemented within current devolved powers or will be at least partially implementable with powers forthcoming under the Smith process. Is it likely that the Scottish Government might act on Atkinson's proposals or at least start to develop policy along similar lines?

Let's start with the one area where genuine progress has been made. As far as is possible under current devolved powers, it would be reasonable for the Scottish Government to claim to have acted upon, or even pre-empted, a number of Atkinson's recommendations which attempt to confront the asymmetries of bargaining power which explain so much of the rise in income inequality. The creation of the Fair Work Convention, National Economic Forum and prioritisation of the living wage sit very comfortably beside Atkinson's calls for a Social and Economic Council and a national pay policy.

But that's about it. Swathes of Atkinson's agenda, particularly around competition, innovation and working towards a new development model and broadening the returns from investment have simply been ignored. Other parts of his admittedly radical agenda only serve to highlight the Scottish Government's apprehension, particularly around tax (where Atkinson proposes a top rate of 65 per cent) and benefits (Atkinson is explicit about what needs to happen: levels should be increased and coverage widened). Atkinson's proposal to abolish the Council Tax and replace with a steeply progressive property tax – a power entirely within the Scottish Government's control since devolution in 1999 – serves to make their current plans look ridiculously weak.

The first report of the Scottish Government's Independent Advisor on Poverty and Inequality published in January 2016 only served to highlight the gap between what is required and the policies we might expect to see in Scotland. This was a report that had nothing original to say or propose about tackling inequality in Scotland. Indeed, the report was largely about poverty reduction. Only one proposal (pay ratio disclosure) could be construed as potentially affecting pay growth at the top.

* * *

Yet there might be some early signs that a more mature approach to tackling inequality might be emerging. Both Labour and the Liberal Democrats have proposed increasing the Scottish Rate of Income Tax to reduce the extent and impact of cuts to local authority budgets. The Scottish Government has dropped its longstanding commitment to cutting corporation tax should the power be forthcoming. The fifth session of the Scottish Parliament is likely to be defined by debates over the wielding of the significant new tax powers arriving 2017 (although it is now possible that the fallout from the European Referendum might supersede tax issues as this Parliament's defining issue). But there's a long way to travel.

This essay has challenged the pre-crisis orthodoxy which sought to explain rising inequality purely in terms of growing global trade and SBTC. However there are compelling reasons to believe that global trends over the coming decades could significantly exacerbate inequality. Increasing automation and digitisation will further undermine the bargaining power of labour and provide massive returns to the owners of the intellectual property.

Therefore, if Scottish politicians are serious about tackling inequality they need to quickly start developing a seriously analytical approach to the subject. Start by assessing Scotland's current position, what is distinct about the UK model and how devolved policy might make an impact. Think through the consequences of current global economic trends and how long term policy development might mitigate adverse impact at Scottish level. Learn from more equal nations but recognise there will be aspects of their models which stem from specific institutional and cultural factors that will be difficult if not impossible to replicate here.

Posturing, sound bites and bad policy are very poor foundations on which to build over the longer term a new Scottish model which should not only be fairer and more equal but resilient and less prone to systemic crises.

Notes

1 Bell, D., Eiser, D., McGoldrick, M. 2014. *Inequality in Scotland: new perspectives*, David Hume Institute

2 Ashcroft, B. *Scottish Economy Watch* blog

3 Piketty, T., 2014. *Capital in the 21st Century*, Harvard University Press (concluding sentence)

4 It is important to acknowledge that new research (Burkhauser, Herault, Jenkins & Wilkins February 2016) *What has been happening to UK income inequality since the mid-1990s? Answers from reconciled and combined household survey and tax return data*. IZA DP no. 9718), published as this chapter was being finalised, challenges the view presented in this paragraph. The study finds that 'there was a marked increase in income inequality in the early 2000s that survey-based estimates do not reveal, and our conclusions are robust to changes in the definitions of income, income-sharing unit, and summary inequality measure'.

5 Hills, J., 2014. *Good Times, Bad Times*, Policy Press

6   Scottish Government. *Reindustrialising Scotland.* June 2014

7   Alvaredo, F., Atkinson, A., Piketty, T., Saez, E. 2013. 'The Top 1% in International and Historical Perspective'. *Journal of Economic Perspectives* – Vol 27, Number 3

8   Galbraith, J., 2012. *Inequality and Instability: a study of the world economy just before the great crisis.* Oxford University Press USA

9   Krugman, p. 2007, *The Conscience of a Liberal.* W.W. Norton and Company

10 Alvaredo, F., Atkinson, A., Piketty, T., Saez, E. 2013. 'The Top 1% in International and Historical Perspective'. *Journal of Economic Perspectives* – Vol 27, Number 3

11 Scotland and the Nordics Part 1 – Tax; STUC Better Way Blog, April 2013

12 Interfluidity: Scale, Progressivity and Socioeconomic Cohesion. 12 October 2014

13 Piketty, T., 2014. 'Income Concentration and Top Income Tax Rates': presentation to USC Tax Policy Conference

14 Alvaredo, F., Atkinson, A., Piketty, T., Saez, E. 2013. 'The Top 1% in International and Historical Perspective'. *Journal of Economic Perspectives* – Vol 27, Number 3

15 Galbraith, J., 2012. *Inequality and Instability: a study of the world economy just before the great crisis.* Oxford University Press USA

16 Bell, B. and Van Reenan, J. 2010. *Bankers' Pay and extreme Wage Inequality in the UK.* Centre for Economic Performance, London School of Economics

17 See for instance Mike Konczal's recent piece 'Frenzied Financialisation', *Washington Monthly* November/December 2014 edition; Thomas Palley's *Financialisation: what it is and why it matters*, Levy Economics Institute Working Paper No. 525 or Galbraith's study cited above.

18 Haldane, A., 2014. Unfair Shares. Bank of England speech, 21 May

19 Levy, F. and Temin, P., 2007. *Inequality and Institutions in 20th Century America.* MIT Department of Economics Working Paper No. 07–17 For an introduction to these ideas see, Centre for Research On Socio-Cultural Change, *Manifesto for the Foundational Economy*, November 2013

20 Galbraith, J., 2012. *Inequality and Instability: a study of the world economy just before the great crisis.* Oxford University Press USA

No Timorous Beasties Here!

GEORGE KEREVAN

What's Wrong with 21st Century Capitalism and how we can fix it

ALL IS NOT well with contemporary capitalism. That's why we need a new political economy. Even on the political right, there is a growing literature analysing what many see as an existential crisis of the system. The neo-liberal model may have conquered all before it in the past 40 years but now it is showing definite signs of fatigue. Most likely we are entering a lengthy period of global deflation similar to the economic climacteric of the 1880s, or the Great Depression of the 1930s, caused by a witches' brew of negative interest rates, over-investment, falling rates of profit, intensified national rivalries and destabilising currency wars.

We are singularly ill-placed to meet this unfolding crisis, intellectually or in policy terms. This is due to a blind acceptance of the prevailing, neo-liberal economic paradigm in academia, the main political parties and the media. Such myopia limits any comprehension of the inherent, entropic tendencies in an economic system that is premised on the illusion of continuous, ever-expanding growth. Put another way, blow a balloon too big and it will burst, even if the balloon is a pretty colour. Policies premised on blowing the global economic balloon ever bigger look eminently rational only until the moment everything goes pop.

Unfortunately, the traditional nostrums of the anti-capitalist left have also failed us as a guide out of the crisis. The historic disaster – in human and material terms – of the Soviet state planning model has disarmed the radical critics of capitalism, who have no notion of what to put in its place. At the same time, the worsening contradictions of contemporary capitalist society – asset bubbles, income disparities, and environmental crises – have circumscribed the traditional social democratic reformist model. This accepts the capitalist growth paradigm ameliorated (ever hopefully) through income redistribution. But the latter is no longer a serious proposition as the high priests of capitalism demand more 'austerity' to 'balance the books'. In the UK, Labour embraced austerity wholeheartedly, presumably as a prelude to re-booting 'growth'. Under the leadership of Ed Miliband and Ed Balls, the party retreated from redistributist social democracy even to the extent of supporting a financial cap on welfare spending, the better to placate the City and the Tory media. The inevitable result was that Labour lost the May 2015 general election. Why vote for Tory lite when you can have the real thing?

So what is the concrete alternative to the failing neo-liberal model on the right and the old Soviet model on the left? For a time, some on the radical left – I include myself in this admonishment – thought the answer lay in a dash for global growth stimulated by the cornucopia of new and 'democratic' technologies that emerged in the 1980s. The Internet would break the economic power of the old capitalist monopolies while the re-entry of the former Communist states into the world market offered a chance to subvert the dominance of US imperialism. In this new economic and political space, a host of small states would emerge to political freedom, including Scotland. These countries would pioneer a fresh and dynamic social democratic model, combining easy direct access to the global market with full employment and liberal (even libertarian) democracy. A new Europe of the Nations, influenced by these smaller member states, would replace the EU of the big bully states and their multinational investors.

Seductive as this 'pragmatic' agenda appeared at the time, we should have known better. There was certainly productivity growth and technological development on an unprecedented scale in the period 1990–2007. The arrival of social media did create a popular alternative to an ideological apparatus controlled by conservative establishment interests. Despite a series of adventurous wars, aided and abetted by the UK, American imperialism failed conspicuously to re-impose the hegemony it had enjoyed in the aftermath of the Second World War. A host of new, vibrant nations emerged to challenge the power of the larger states. In Scotland, a re-awakened sense of nationhood led to the return of a devolved parliament and near victory for the Yes camp in the September 2014 independence referendum.

Yet overall the economic, environmental and social balance sheet of the period 1989–2008 is largely negative – and for reasons that should have been apparent in advance. The only excuse I can give for my own short-sightedness is that the failure of the anti-Stalinist Marxist left – from the 1960s onwards – to develop a coherent economic alternative, made it all too attractive to try and tame the free market tiger. But tamed it would not, and could not be. By 2008, a host of ills re-emerged straight from the classic textbooks of both Marx and Keynes, leading to the worst financial crisis since the 1930s. Soon bad political choices followed bad economic ones. The Credit Crunch of 2007–08 was swiftly followed by the implosion in the Eurozone. When Germany's profligate banks were threatened by collapse as a result of importunate lending, Berlin imposed an insane austerity regime on the debtor states of the Mediterranean south – repeating the exact mistake of deliberate deflation condemned by John Maynard Keynes in 1936. The Anglo-Saxons avoided this economic insanity only by printing money. But rather than use this extra aggregate demand to restructure their economies towards something sustainable, or to relieve poverty, the US and UK invented 'quantitative easing' – using the new money to fund a boom in stock market prices, triggering another inevitable asset bubble. Initially China pursued a different path, using a Keynesian-style fiscal stimulus to boost growth, thereby temporarily providing Western economies with a market for their industrial exports, and developing economies with a market for raw material exports. By 2015 the Chinese boomlet was over, strangled by over-capacity, inflation, excess debt and rampant corruption. Finally, a global collapse in commodity prices, static productivity and flatlining of wages tripped the world economy into a permanent deflation. The vote in the UK in June 2016 to quit the EU signalled a political end to the era of globalisation and the return of a 1930s-style period of trade wars and competitive devaluations.

Despite these extraordinary developments, and nearly a decade into the systemic crisis provoked by the 2008 banking failures, the international left has struggled to come forth with any comprehensive alternative to the free-market model. Far less has it found a reply to the prevailing 'austerity' policies pursued by Western governments. This lack is not down to a failure of intellectual brilliance, far less any shortage of books on the crisis. Rather, it stems from a lack of practice. In short, the left has stopped experimenting in the real world. We lack bold initiatives from local councils, from socialist or green administrations, from workers' cooperatives and from trades unions; initiatives that would test new ways of creating sustainable employment, training workers, ending housing shortages, funding useful social investment, producing things that matter, raising incomes and ending poverty.

Such an experimental alternative is not only necessary but eminently possible. My agenda here is not to suggest some solution *sui generis* to the crisis of the free market system – which would be a ridiculous conceit. Rather it is to sketch out some of the concrete problems that need to be addressed in the operation of existing capitalism, and to advance some specific reforms that could be implemented experimentally here in Scotland by a Scottish government or local councils. In other words, to develop the beginnings of a new political economy using Scotland as a laboratory – an agenda that rejects not simply the neo-liberal variant of capitalism but the entire system itself. I begin with a caveat: Scotland, with a population of just over five million, remains a tiny cog in the vast capitalist wheel. Any political discourse that starts by trying to ignore this reality is doomed to irrelevance and utopianism. That is not a counsel of despair. Nor is it an appeal for a flaccid reformism. Instead, it is an argument for picking a fight we can win.

This approach is coloured by two axioms. First, capitalism is a human artefact, and what humans create they can also modify.

Curiously, though we associate the term 'capitalism' with Karl Marx, he never used it. The word was actually invented by the novelist William Makepeace Thackeray in 1854, in the novel *The Newcomes*. The plot focuses on the eponymous Newcome family and their rise to wealth, as the family eventually marry into the aristocracy. Thackeray treats his hero, Colonel Newcome, as the very model of the rising Victorian bourgeois class: respectable, hardworking, and religious. But in the end, the Colonel is ruined in a banking crash – *plus ça change*. As with Thackeray, we need to understand that the capitalist system is not an act of God, or a force of nature, or quintessentially perfect. It is a product of human calculation created over the past half millennium. What humans invent, they can change if it does not suit them, no matter how complicated the process involved.

Second, I agree with Karl Marx on the left and Friedrich Hayek on the right, that human societies are not the result of philosophical blueprints but evolve over time through a process of trial and error, social conflict and political argument. No one knows for sure what will emerge from the current contradictions of the capitalist system. The solution is to follow the advice of the Brazilian progressive philosopher Roberto Unger and experiment.[1] What eventually succeeds we will only discover as we go along, albeit through a process of deliberate human intervention. The point is to be creative rather than didactic. This is a message that does not come easily to the left.

So here follows some modest economic proposals that could be applied by a progressive government at Holyrood. We focus on three concrete developments that signpost the end of the neo-liberal era: (1) a growing glut of investment capital that is causing permanent financial bubbles; (2) stalled real incomes for the mass of the population in the West; and (3) the potential for a great labour shake out involving the loss of professional jobs to the next generation of computers. We will examine what might be done practically in a Home Rule Scotland to ameliorate or (more properly) subvert the impact of these accumulating problems. The aim is to embed a non-capitalist economic practice inside the belly of the whale. Such an outcome will not be stable. There will be social friction and resistance from the prevailing capitalist order. But from the experiment will come new ways of responding to the existential failure of the existing economic paradigm – and with that comes hope. This is not an abstract agenda. The world now faces a new era of deflation, low productivity growth, and even a regression in incomes in middle rank, developing economies. Finding an alternative political economy has never been more necessary.

Part One: The Problems

Problem One: Too Much Capital

To be concrete, we need to understand how existing capitalism operates. Sociologically, of course, it remains at heart a social system with unique economic classes, power relationships, sexual division, state machinery, laws, repressive apparatus, urban compounds and cultural artifice. But fundamentally it is a system historically focused on one thing only: accumulating capital for its own sake, and in perpetuity. Let us note at the outset that capital itself is not a set of assets or a sum of money. Rather (and this is Marx's unique insight) capital is a social relationship which gives some people private entitlements to command future economic resources. But there is more: capitalism, as an economic system, is geared to expanding those entitlements infinitely. Which makes it a permanent growth machine.

Note: capitalism is not synonymous with markets or trading. This is a mistake the left makes all too easily. Humans have always voluntarily exchanged the fruits of their labour, be it in local barter markets or through complex, long-range trade routes going back millennia. After sex, markets are what define human society. Capitalism is something different than buying and selling as an act. But capitalism is unique in that it commodifies absolutely everything, starting with human labour power. This allows labour, land and physical resources to be purchased (using existing 'capital') and concentrated to produce commodities that can be sold for the highest return, thereby yielding yet more capital. And so we have our permanent growth machine, the only one in human history.

The advantages of the capitalist system, compared with all previous economic models, are immediately obvious. This perpetual growth machine spews out an ever-expanding hoard of commodities (goods and services) that have made the average citizen of North America, Australasia, Europe or South Asia richer than the kings of old. Taking annual GDP as a proxy for commodities (though not necessarily well-being) real global production was flat till around 1350, and then started accelerating. It doubled between 1350 and 1650; then doubled again by 1800. In the 120 years between 1800 and 1920, world output increased by the power of ten. In the next 60 years to 1980, it multiplied by another factor of ten. Even after the recent crash, global output is two and a half times what it was in 1980. Compared with previous economic systems, capitalism wins hands down in terms of productive efficiency. And while it does not manufacture goods and services except as a by-product of capital accumulation, the sheer cornucopia of commodities beats the lack of them in most people's estimation.

There are other social and cultural advantages associated with capitalism, at least compared with its historical predecessors. While most labour power is commodified in capitalism, complex industrial systems require skilled voluntary rather than slave labour. Besides, extracting profits requires the capitalist to sell consumer goods on a vast scale. This necessitates a willing mass market that is incompatible with extreme poverty or draconian state repression. In the late 19th century, capitalists also learned that the organised labour movement was in a good position to extract economic and political concessions or else disrupt the system, Samson-like. The result was social democracy and variations on the welfare state.

But something has changed for the worse in the capitalism of the 21st century. The central problem is that the system is finally generating more profits than it can safely or purposefully use, at least with the returns demanded by the investing class. Despite the financial wizardry – or quackery – of the financial system to absorb this money, the supply of capital has outstripped growth in the underlying real economy. Put simply, modern capitalism is afflicted with financial obesity. Despite near-zero interest levels, despite the recent banking crisis, and despite much reduced economic growth, the global savings rate – a proxy for the surplus capital available for reinvestment each year – has risen to a record 25 per cent of world GDP. Some apologists argue that there is no true 'glut' of capital but merely one of governments printing (electronically) excess money. Certainly, there's a lot of that going on too, but there is no gainsaying the fact that accumulated financial assets represent getting on for ten times annual global GDP. These assets represent a claim on future GDP and ten into one does not go. Worse: we can expect a further 50 per cent rise in total available stock of capital by 2020, to a staggering $900 trillion. Much of this increase will come from China. The problem is: how does this money capital get reinvested? Answer: when too much capital is chasing too few returns, people take undue risks and financial bubbles form. The result is the inherent and perpetual financial instability that characterises the contemporary capitalist system.

Up till the 1970s, governments imposed restrictions on capital export. But globalisation, allied to new technology, has unleashed the financial floodgates. The explosive growth in mobile financial capital has caused a precipitous drop in real (risk-adjusted) returns on physical and intangible assets, as too much capital chases too few high return investments. But worse: the desperate search for the highest returns has encouraged lunatic risk-taking: the Japanese real-estate bubble of the 1980s, the US dot-com bubble of the 1990s; more recently, the American and British property bubble of the early millennium, which transmuted into the global bank crash; and lately the Chinese property bubble. The consequences are not just rampant financial instability and permanent crisis. As the real rate of return on productive investments declines, pensioners will have less to live on.

Of course, people have been predicting a glut of capital since capitalism was invented. In the 19th century, Marx predicted the ever-growing accumulation of capital would drive down the rate of profit till the system simply broke down and the workers took over. However, periodic economic crises served to reduce the capital surplus by bankrupting individual capitalist investors, while war and technological development created new investment opportunities at a higher rate of profit. Existential crisis postponed, so to speak. Politically, the system has also gotten better at trying to head off collapse. The state has stepped in to borrow a proportion of the surplus and use it to bolster consumer demand while simultaneously providing a market for infrastructure and military products with a guaranteed rate of profit. But we are nearing the end of that wheeze, as the cost of servicing national debt through taxation has reached penal rates. Above all, since the dot-com bubble collapsed in 2000, central banks have learned to print money (aka 'quantitative easing') to buy bonds and force down interest rates to near zero. This has the short term effect of providing a market outlet for the glut of savings – investors can buy bonds with their excess capital, safe in the knowledge the central bank is propping up their value using the newly printed cash. And by keeping interest rates at zero, while flooding the banks with liquidity, we also create a demand for company shares – hence the boom in global stock markets since 2010, despite the world recession. Capitalist investors thus avoid bankruptcy and even feel richer – unlike the mass of unemployed youth around the globe.

If there is all glut of capital around, how come small firms and mortgage seekers are having such a hard time accessing it? After the credit crunch – caused by insane practices in the derivatives market – politicians have been forcing banks to hold more and more capital as security. As a result, bank lending has been deliberately constrained in Europe and America. Put another way: we might have low interest rates, but regulations requiring lenders to hold more security has ensured small firms can't access the cash – especially as those small firms are routinely designated by banks and regulators as the riskiest organisations to lend to. At the same time, large industrial companies that can generate investment cash of their own (usually by selling bonds) are increasingly unwilling to put it to productive use because returns are deemed too poor. US multinationals have around $1 trillion hoarded overseas. Apple has a staggering $130 billion sitting in offshore accounts. If American companies bring their earnings home to redistribute to shareholders, the revenue is taxed. So instead they are using the money to buy back their own shares.

We now reach the nub of the irrationality of neo-liberal capitalism: while the global economy is accumulating more capital than business wishes to use in current market circumstances, there is no shortage of genuine need in the world – for clean water, for renewable energy, for better health care, for healthy food, for literacy, for higher education, or for decent housing. Equally, while there is an irreducible minimum of working hours required to sustain productive output, and while many folk actually like to be occupied, there is an unmet demand for more leisure. Put simply, the market definition of a useful financial return is at odds with social need. This is hardly a new problem with capitalism. What is new is the scale of the dysfunction. We have an historically unique glut of capital seeking an outlet, yet it is either being sat on (metaphorically) or used in reckless financial speculation that keeps threatening to destroy the banking system. What can be done? More to the point, what can we do in tiny Scotland? But before we can address possible solutions, we need to factor in another structural defect in contemporary capitalism: the failure of wages to rise in line with economic growth.

Problem Two: Too Meagre Wages

Wages as a share of national income are falling significantly throughout industrial capitalism. In the advanced OECD economies, the wage share has fallen on average from 73 per cent of GDP in 1980 to 64 per cent in 2007, at the onset of the global recession. Overall, real wage growth has lagged behind productivity growth since around 1980.[2] This constitutes a major historical change, as wage shares were stable or increasing in the post-war era as urbanisation spread and strong industrial trades unions enjoyed significant bargaining power. In the Anglo-Saxon countries in particular, a sharp polarisation of personal income distribution has occurred. Top income earners have increased their income share dramatically. In the United States, the top one per cent of the income distribution increased their share of national income by more than ten percentage points in the recent period. Yet even in Germany the bottom of the income distribution has lost ground, as the share of non-managerial wage earners in national income has decreased sharply. This increase in inequality is being driven by changes in the remuneration of bankers and senior managers, whose bonuses are counted as labour compensation (ie wages) in National Accounts. If bonuses were counted as part of profits, as was the case in the 19th century, the compression of wages as a share of GDP would be even more pronounced. The social and economic impact of this falling share of wages is both. In the long term it is stoking social unrest. If workers cannot share in the returns from investment and productivity, why should they actively support the system? In the short run, the falling share of wages in GDP is forcing households into increasing levels of debt in order to maintain and improve living standards. This adds to the financial instabilities of capitalism; eg housing bubbles.

What has caused this squeeze on wages? Clearly many factors are involved, including loss of trades union bargaining power, technological change displacing skilled workers, and increased global competition. But the most thorough studies suggest that financialisation has had the largest negative impact, explaining more than half of the total change of the wage share. The burgeoning role of the financial sector is the hallmark of the transformations of economy and society since the mid-1970s. But this divorce of finance capital from industrial capital is just another way of describing (in institutional terms) the emerging glut of capital relative to productive investment outlets. Pension funds, hedge funds, investment banks, private equity funds and the like invest in financial assets, chasing higher returns than productivity growth in the real economy can supply. The ratio of capital to income will rise without limit as long as financial rates of return are significantly higher than the economy's rate of growth of productivity. Occasionally and exceptionally, economic crises have destroyed capital, delaying the imbalance. It was further delayed by exceptionally high returns to industrial investment in post-war America and Europe (which raised wage shares in passing). But the normal cycle of unrestrained capital growth has now reasserted itself, helped by the elimination of Stalinism in Russia and China, and by the use of quantitative easing by central banks. Quantitative easing has funded a gigantic bubble in share values, thus preventing the destruction of individual wealth following the 2008 financial crash. Result: capital accumulation is once again outstripping industrial investment, depressing the share of wages.

The huge rise in bonus earnings at the top of the income distribution range is another side effect, adding to inequality. In the United States, the richest one per cent appropriated 60 per cent of the increase in US national income between 1977 and 2007. Technology and globalisation can hardly explain this. Nor can classical bourgeois economic theory which maintains that pay is determined by the employee's marginal productivity. To suggest that the marginal productivity of senior bankers has skyrocketed is to invite ridicule, especially in the aftermath of the 2007 financial crisis. Rather, we are seeing a small number of individuals exploiting the system within the financial sector to pay themselves sums that bear no relationship to effort, justified only by excessive risk taking (aka speculating and gambling). This process is accelerated by the fall in marginal income tax rates in Western countries since the 1980s, which have increased the incentive to bargain for astronomically higher pay.

The historic rise in the share of income appropriated by the super-rich at the start of the 21st century – a direct result of neo-liberal economic policy – is important for more than reasons of equity or morality. It has also resulted in a dearth of effective demand. Put simply, the mass of ordinary workers and consumers increasingly lack the collective spending power to purchase what they are employed to make, unless they resort to debt finance. But we are now at an economic crossroads. Consumer debt in the Western word has reached unsustainable levels. At the same time, the onset of global deflation, combined with the failure of zero-bound interest rates to produce growth, means the international economy is desperate for a new source of stimulus. That can only come from wages and/or public spending.

Problem three: too few jobs

A third existential crisis for capitalism is now beckoning to add to the glut of capital and the decline in the wage share: the next generation seems likely to face the horrendous prospect of the mass deskilling of professional labour as a result of 'smart' machines.

Traditionally, the way workers tried to socialise the operation of capitalism (aka the commodification of labour time) was to fight to reduce the length of the working week. Robert Owen famously instituted the ten-hour day at his socialist enterprise at New Lanark in Scotland, and by 1817 was campaigning for an eight-hour day under the slogan: Eight hours labour, Eight hours recreation, Eight hours rest. The International Workingmen's Association took up the demand for an eight-hour day in 1866, declaring: 'The legal limitation of the working day is a preliminary condition without which all further attempts at improvements and emancipation of the working class must prove abortive'. In fact, the 40-hour week was not standard in the industrial capitalist world till the mid 20th century, with the general dissemination of mass production techniques. But since then, attempts to reduce the formal working week further have stalled, though the 'informal' domestic work week has been dramatically shortened by household appliances. For instance, though France formally introduced a legal 35-hour week in 1998, the de facto French workweek for full-time employees exceeds an average of 39.5 hours, as a result of loopholes.

This is a highly unexpected outcome. In 1930, John Maynard Keynes predicted that technological advancement would mean a workweek of just 15 hours a week. That same year, biologist Julian

Huxley predicted the two-day workweek. 'The human being can consume so much and no more,' Huxley said in 1930. 'When we reach the point when the world produces all the goods that it needs in two days, as it inevitably will, we must curtail our production of goods and turn our attention to the great problem of what to do with our new leisure.' As late as 1965, a US Senate subcommittee predicted a 14-hour workweek by the year 2000.

Why has the tendency to reduce the working week ground to a halt despite a massive increase in productive capacity? Mainstream economics has come up with a number of explanations. One is the demand for paid employment has increased as people try to achieve the standard of living promoted by contemporary cultural (and commercial norms). This process is reinforced by social changes such as the rise of one-parent families. Again, there has been a transformation of the work pattern, with a core of highly paid, highly-skilled professional and technical jobs supported by burgeoning part time and self-employed sectors, especially since the crisis of 2008. The latter workers are generally much less well paid and less secure. Finally, there is the possibility that, for core production activities, it is simply organisationally difficult or inconvenient to reduce labour time much below 40 hours per week, without disrupting communications and contacts in the work place. For instance, a network of 100 people working 40 hours each per week is easier to manage than one of 400 people working ten hours each per week.

However, while these explanations have some credence, they miss out a reality embedded deep in how the cycle of capital accumulation actually works. Investing in new technology is expensive. As a result, each wave of new technical development forces companies to try and recoup their heavy capital outlay faster than ever. In other words, technical change tends to speed up the turnover time of capital investment. That, in turn, necessitates an intensification of the work process. In other words, technological progress – far from reducing the notional working week – actually intensifies the nature of work practices.

We have abundant evidence of this happening following the

economic and banking crisis. In the UK, the number of people working more than 48 hours per week jumped by 15 per cent since 2010 (to 3,417,000). In fact, full time employees in the UK work longer hours than any EU country bar Greece and Austria; the average working week is now 42.7 hours. Even this is an underestimate. Young professionals in service industries, especially in London, feel pressured to stay after their contractual work hours or risk being seen as unambitious or disloyal to the company. A YouGov poll found that 67 per cent of those aged between 18 and 26 regularly stayed late at the office. In the United States, the situation is even worse with 18 per cent of full time employees working 60 hours or more each week.

This development implies that the binary split between highly paid, full time workers and lower paid, part time staff could be permanent. Further, it suggests that any future gains in productivity will accrue in higher wages to the specialist workers, still working circa 40 hours per week. Meanwhile, workers in part time jobs will find their real incomes static because it is more difficult to introduce productivity gains in (largely) service sectors, at least without eliminating the need for such workers altogether (eg replacing call centres with computers). In Scotland, we can already see these trends at work. The core professional group is smaller than in England. Currently, there are only some 14,000 Scots earning over the £150,000 top 'additional' rate threshold (latest figures available: 2013–14). That is barely one half of one per cent of all Scottish taxpayers. And only some 8.5 per cent of taxpayers north of the border pay the 40 per cent middle class professional rate, compared with 14.7 per cent in the UK as a whole.

But 21st century capitalism faces a further threat to its stability: the displacement by 'smart' machines of middle class employees in high-earning professional jobs involving the collation, analysis and dissemination of information. Such jobs – in banks, offices, media bureaux and government departments – are about to go the way of navvies, shorthand typists or telephone operators. Companies such as Google are already funding new technology that will not simply collect and process information, but draw inferences, answer questions, publish journals and articles and even make recommendations. The threat stretches beyond white-collar jobs. Versatile robots are starting to takeover over many types of routine manual work in areas such as packaging, sorting and delivery. McKinsey, the management consultancy, estimates that by 2025, productivity gains in 'knowledge work' (ranging from clerical to professional services) using smart technology will threaten 40 per cent of all the current office jobs. At the same time, the average price of high-precision robots used in production will become cheap. As a result, these robots will jeopardise 25 million to 40 million blue collar jobs in developed countries and 15 million to 35 million in developing ones. Of course, we've heard such threats before but global economic growth and demands for new kinds of skilled labour have always outpaced the destruction of older industrial ecologies. However, this time round, a combination of the Internet, new technology, access to mass data sources online, and – above all – the cheapness and ubiquity of intelligent machines, could bring the biggest jobs cull ever. In law and medicine, machines are likely to produce better answers than humans, who struggle to keep up with the latest research. At the same time, breakthroughs in computer vision mean that low-skilled manual work is no longer too hard to automate. For instance, weeding machines are now smart enough to pick their way through a field without harming the crop.

The prospect of a large-scale cull of jobs in the next generation has been examined in a path-breaking study by Carl Benedikt Frey and Michael Osborne, of the Martin School at Oxford University.[3] Frey and Osborne return to the scenario that sudden technological change in capitalism could catapult us into a situation where there is a replacement of a significant numbers of jobs. They provide a highly detailed analysis of where the job losses are likely to occur, ranking them by probability. They forecast that 47 per cent of jobs in the United States are vulnerable to such technological change.

If we apply the Frey-Osborne analysis to Scotland, the results are disturbing because of the relatively lower proportion of high-level workers in the economy. The occupational categories in Scotland vulnerable to computerisation by mid century are in sales (172,000 workers), administration (263,000), process operators (134,000), personal services (202,000) and skilled trades (236,000). That's circa one million jobs with an 80 per cent chance of being done by machines in the coming generation – a chilling prospect for a small nation. It raises two questions. First, where will Scotland find new jobs? But secondly, are we not faced with the need to redefine the very nature of productive employment itself? Has the time come to 'de-commodify' labour, if not wholly, then at least to some degree?

Part Two: Experimental Solutions

We now come to solutions, especially those that could be experimented with at a Scottish level and within the inevitable constraints imposed by global capitalism. Is there a way we can curb the glut of capital while raising real wages and generating meaningful employment? Can we escape the logic of unrestrained capital accumulation for its own sake?

A tax on capital

There is an obvious way to mitigate the social costs of asset bubbles: introduce a tax on excess holdings of capital; ie tax wealth? To suggest such a thing in the era of neo-liberalism is to risk ridicule, or at least to have one's sanity questioned. After all, surely wealth begets investment, begets jobs? To tax wealth is surely to tax the investment goose that lays the employment egg. From the perspective of received economic wisdom, a wealth tax seems almost perverse. Yet go back to the 1940s and you will find the great economist John Maynard Keynes solemnly advocating a tax on wealth as a means of funding post-war reconstruction by raiding unproductive capital in the hands of the rentier class.[4] Keynes argued that a modest wealth tax also minimised income tax and therefore boosted effective demand as a counter to deflation (something we could use now). Even that arch free-marketeer and libertarian Friedrich Hayek flirted with the idea of a wealth tax in the early 1940s, as the least distorting way to pay off the National Debt – George Osborne please note. Who are we to disagree with such eminent supporters of capitalism?

Taxes on capital come in three kinds: (1) taxes on profit streams, at a company level, before or after distribution; (2) taxes on capital gains; and (3) taxes on gross wealth itself, usually via death duties.

Start with taxing profits; ie taxing the return to capital. Traditionally, this is done though Corporation Tax (CT). Perhaps the very simplest way of taxing excess wealth balances is to raise the existing rate of CT. During the period when George Osborne was Chancellor, he reduced the headline rate to 20 per cent, and proposed (before being fired by Theresa May) to go even lower as a response to Brexit. However, in Germany, the equivalent of CT is significantly higher than in the UK yet both capital investment and productivity growth are also higher. Why? Partly because Germany invests in public infrastructure, which boosts private industrial productivity. And partly because cuts in UK headline CT have been offset by rises in other business taxes which create worse market distortions. In 2007, for instance, Gordon Brown cut the headline rate of CT paid by big firms from 30 per cent to 28 per cent, but cynically raised the rate for smaller firms from 19 per cent to 22 per cent. Out of the total tax contribution paid by UK business firms in 2013, only 26 per cent (£39bn) was from CT, the other three quarters coming from Employers National Insurance (£59bn), business rates (£26bn), and fuel duties (around £13bn). This shift falls most heavily on small and medium sized business for which labour and property costs are proportionately higher. This should not surprise us: the largest one per cent of companies pay 81 per cent of all UK corporation tax, so they have been lobbying hard to shift the tax burden onto other firms. Unfortunately, this is squeezing job and investment prospects in SMEs. Might it not be less distorting to tax profits at a higher rate rather than inputs such as labour and property? The US federal corporate tax rate is 35 per cent, a good deal higher than the 20 per cent scheduled for the UK in 2015. Yet America's record in high technology is much better than in the UK. If

Corporation Tax is raised within the tax mix, provided labour taxes are reduced, and provided tax incentives are put in place to encourage domestic saving and investment, any apparent downside can be minimised.

This line of reasoning has direct implications for SNP policy. During the referendum campaign, Alex Salmond argued in favour of cutting CT after independence: '… this will increase revenues, increase wealth, increase jobs and make us able to afford to do things like pay carers a decent amount, to abolish the bedroom tax and introduce the socially progressive policies on which we stand.' But the post-Credit Crunch economic universe has subverted the traditional Laffer Curve argument in important ways. To start with, non-bank companies in the UK and US are sitting on historically large piles of free cash. Cutting corporate taxes only adds to this cash mountain, not to productive investment. Indeed, if the money is dispersed it is to fund share buy-backs, which are now running at record levels. There is a disturbing conclusion to be drawn from this corporate cash Everest: it is prima face evidence of monopoly and inefficiency. Standard neo-classical economics textbooks will tell you that competition should erode excess profits, passing efficiency gains to the consumer. If corporations are amassing more money than they can use, this suggests monopoly is rife in the economy. Conclusion: any progressive Scottish government needs to turn its attention to supply-side measures that boost competition and make investment in manufacturing attractive. Devolving CT to Holyrood only makes policy sense if it is used differentially as part of a plan to encourage domestic expansion in particular industrial sectors, or as a counter-cyclical measure. It should not be used as a crude bribe to secure inward investment, a policy that in the post-Credit Crunch era will penalise tax revenues for no marginal gain. Since Nicola Sturgeon became SNP leader, there are signs the party has moved away from its earlier stance of cutting CT. But is it radical enough to raise CT, while reducing taxes on employing labour?

We should also note here that the current form of CT is flawed. We can tax profits in a much more socially efficient manner. The Institute of Fiscal Studies recommends a number of ways the tax system could be reformed to boost productive investment and labour productivity.[5] Top of the list is the introduction of an allowance for corporate equity, known as ACE. An ACE is an allowance for the opportunity cost of equity finance similar to the deduction already given for the costs of debt finance (ie interest payments). Introducing an ACE makes long term equity investments more attractive vis-à-vis debt finance invented through the banking system, especially if interest rate deductions are reduced and there are tax concessions for keeping money locked in manufacturing investment. The use of an ACE still offers concessions to capital but does so in a manner that discourages speculative borrowing while encouraging productive investment. A future Scottish Government that has control over CT should consider this reform.

What about taxes on capital gains? CGT is a tax on the increase in the value of an asset between its acquisition and its disposal. The problem with taxing the capital gain is that we are taxing people who are trying to get rich by investing, instead of just taxing very rich people. This leads to governments introducing complicated exemptions and loopholes that make capital gains taxes (especially in Britain) prime game for tax avoidance. Besides, investments can soar in value for decades without gains ever being realized or tax ever coming due. The (untaxed) capital stays in the financial system, helping to stoke asset bubbles. Amazingly, when those assets are passed finally to heirs, the unrealized gains can simply disappear for capital-gains-tax purposes, if you get a good accountant. GCT also causes economic distortions. By far the biggest exemption from CGT in the UK is the rise in the value of main homes. This is estimated to have cost the Treasury over £17bn in 2008, at the top of the last housing bubble. That was more than three times the total CGT yield.

British Chancellors have struggled to reform CGT in order to encourage longer term investing but the results have only complicated this tax further. As a result, many economists in Britain and America have long favoured scraping CGT altogether. Perhaps a more courageous approach would be to keep a highly simplified, moderate but ruthlessly effective taxation of capital income. This would be combined with a moderate but effective taxation of inheritance. The overall aim would be to bring capital gains back into the tax base, either during the course of an investor's life or at their death. Some taxation of any increase in house values would need to be included. This would be unpopular, of course. However, by exempting rising property prices from capital gains, we have massively distorted savings flows away from productive investment. In addition, we have contributed to house price bubbles, not to mention the creation of a wealth divide between those on the property ladder and those too poor to climb on. Admittedly, electoral politics make taxing gains in house values difficult – though it has recently been introduced, north and south of the border, for property bought for rent. It is a question of starting the process.

Apologists for the neo-liberal model will argue that such a tougher CGT regime will drain capital out of the investment system. In the long-run, according to this view, the national capital investment fund would drain out, like water from a bath, till it reached zero (aka the famous Chamley-Judd theory, which is used to justify zero tax on capital). But this only happens if you posit extremely unlikely conditions. For a start, provided governments have a rule that CGT revenues are returned to the national investment pool through public capital programmes, no such leakage occurs. Second, mainstream bourgeois economists claim that taxing capital through a CGT is distorting because it encourages immediate consumption while reducing long term productivity, thereby making economic decisions sub-optimal. But this view assumes there is indeed an 'optimal' economic nirvana in which society has already chosen its preferred trade-off between consumption and investment (saving). On the contrary, people constantly vary their capital accumulation over time, to amass a pension pot, as deferred consumption, or for security (especially in Asia). As a result, there is no clear way 'society' can ever know or compute its preferred 'substitution' between consumption and investment. So arguing that zero capital taxes are somehow 'optimal' is both utopian and self-serving. Which means an effective CGT is justified by the life

cycle nature of saving and investment in order to smooth out investment gluts and famines.

An alternative to the CGT is a pure wealth tax levied not realized
capital but on gross capital assets. The French economist Thomas
Piketty [6] proposes a global progressive wealth tax of up to two per
cent on net assets above $5 million.[6] A global wealth tax would elim-
inate distortions in allocation between nations, as the same tax would
prevail everywhere. The practical problem for such a tax (as Pikettty
accepts) would be in getting universal agreement to impose and
collect it. The same goes for variations of the so-called Tobin Tax,
first proposed by the economist and Nobel Laureate James Tobin,
which proposes some form of levy on international financial transactions; Eg on short term currency flows or the international sale of
broader classes of assets such as stocks, bonds, commodities, and
derivatives. A group of key Eurozone countries, including Germany
and France, is pushing forward with a scheme to introduce a tax on
cross-border financial transactions despite threats by the UK to block
the project by recourse to the Court of Justice. The details of this
so-called Financial Transactions Tax remain sketchy. Even if approved,
it seems unlikely to be levied on a scale that would prick an asset
bubble.

If capital taxes remain a distant prospect at a global or regional
bloc level, is there a possibility a small country could impose one by
itself without losing foreign investment or harming rates of saving?
In fact, one successful Western country does have a wealth tax: the
Netherlands, which is hardly an example of either poverty or industrial inefficiency. The Netherlands makes life simple by being one of
the few Western industrial nations to forego a complicated CGT. The
Netherlands taxes gross capital assets, not realised capital gains.
Assets in excess of a basic minimum (€21,139 in 2012) are taxed. A
standard yield on such wealth (four per cent, based on low-risk bonds)
is imputed. If you invest in riskier assets, you gain. A fixed 30 per cent
of the assumed yield is taxed at a flat rate of 1.2 per cent. There are
several advantages to this system. First, it is neutral between invest-

ment decisions. Next, it is easy to comply with for both taxpayers and tax administrators, while revenues are less volatile. Why could Scotland not introduce a modest wealth tax on the Dutch model?

If Scotland introduces a wealth tax, or a range of tax measures aimed at capturing a larger share of profits for public use, there will be an inevitable response from the business class and rich that such a move will hurt 'incentives', discourage inward investment and 'force' high net wealth individuals to migrate. Some domestic wealth holders may leave but they can hardly take their landed property with them – they can only sell it on. Any loss of tax revenues from higher-paid individuals can (and will) be off-set by the economic stimulus resulting from transferring unproductive wealth into public investment. As for inward investment, that goes where it can link easily into global supply chains, find a skilled workforce, and operate in a safe environment – which is why Scotland is a magnet for such footloose capital. For multinational manufacturers, the local marginal rate of business tax is of secondary importance. Otherwise, Asian and US multinationals would not be in, say, France. However, it is important to stress that any taxation of capital (in whatever form) should not be used to fund revenue spending or consumption. My preference is to use it to reduce the National Debt (primarily in good times) and support infrastructure spending (primarily in downswings).

Active Labour Market Policies

We turn now to the twin issues of raising the wage share and creating socially useful employment. Interfering in the labour market is supposed to be a bad idea, especially if it limits bankers' bonuses. However, once you accept that labour markets don't work efficiently, the door is open to making them function better. The argument against what economists call Active Labour Market Policies (ALMPS) is that they distort the proper allocation of resources and reduce economic efficiency. But is this true in practice? The evidence suggests the conventional economic paradigm of how labour markets operate is wrong. Conventional wisdom has it that workers are paid what they contribute to production (their 'marginal product'). If true, the only way to raise real wages is through raising productivity. As (in the current paradigm) market de-regulation leads to productivity gains through competition, so governments should keep out of the labour market lest they impoverish the workforce. Of course, reality shows this neat syllogism is self-serving, ideological nonsense.

Consider a practical example. Employment in Scotland contracted by 4.7 per cent at the depth of the recent recession but fell by only 2.5 per cent in the UK. While English firms hoarded labour, Scottish firms were quicker to downsize. From a capitalist point of view, Scottish firms were making themselves meaner and leaner. You can see this by the fact that productivity in Scotland shot up – more was being made with fewer workers. Scottish productivity rose to 99.3 per cent of the UK average in 2010, up from a miserly 94.0 per cent in 2003. By 2012, Scottish output per hour actually matched the UK level. Improved productivity should, all things being equal, lead to workers being paid more. But the evidence in Scotland and England does not bear this out over the crisis period. Earnings in Scotland have remained stubbornly below the UK average. In 2013, despite productivity catching up, full time gross median, full-time earnings in Scotland were only £508.30p a week, compared with £517.50p for the UK. By 2015, the gap had narrowed to £527 per week in Scotland versus £528 across the UK. But the fact remains that while Scottish workers were delivering greater productivity, a wages gap remained with the rest of the UK. This is due in part to the fact that Scottish wage rates in manufacturing are held down by global competition with Asia. But it also indicates that earnings don't equate to marginal productivity as orthodox economic argues, except maybe – a very big maybe – with a long lag, and usually only with a significant 'push' from the trades unions. All of which suggests there might be a case for Active Labour Market intervention.

Pricing people into work

In the neo-liberal paradigm, taxes are seen as a bad thing. Curiously, there is one exception to this rule – employment. In the UK we levy substantial, regressive taxes on both hiring and on taking a job. These taxes are called (erroneously) 'national insurance' contributions (NI). In fact they are a straight levy on income and profits that goes straight to the UK Exchequer. Putting more folk back into socially productive work and increasing the share of wages in National Income starts with removing this ideological anomaly. Manipulating the existing National Insurance system could prove a handy tool, which is why we should campaign to have its operation devolved to Scotland.

At best, employee NI contributions provide necessary public revenues while keeping down the headline rate of income tax. This serves to bamboozle employees into believing they are paying less income tax than they are. The employer's NI contributions also enrich the Treasury and help pay for an education system that supports industry, which is to the good. But the cost is levied regardless of business efficiency or worker productivity, which is a negative.

This raises the obvious question: why not reform the tax system to encourage hiring? In fact, the principle was embraced by George Osborne, when he was Chancellor. In April 2014, Osborne introduced a so-called an employment allowance that removes the first £2,000 from employers' NI contributions. Much given to hyperbole, Osborne called his move 'the largest tax cut in the budget'. He claimed that, as a result, a third of employers in the UK would pay 'no jobs tax at all'. However, what chancellors give with one hand, they have a habit of snatching back surreptitiously with the other. The NI reform was introduced in the same 2013 budget that cut corporation tax for big companies but not for SMEs. That effectively shifted the relative burden of corporation tax on to the SME sector. Again, in 2010, the then Coalition Government trumpeted a plan for a 'holiday' in employer NI for SMEs in a number of specified regions, if they took on 'new labour'. Osborne claimed 400,000 businesses would benefit. But hidden in the small print was the requirement for each firm to apply specifically for the reduction. The application process proved to be too bureaucratic and complicated. Result: far fewer businesses applied than had been anticipated.

The point about these earlier labour market reforms is that they were piece-meal, limited in operation, and still accepted the underlying logic of taxing hiring rather than the excess of capital in the system. What's the alternative? A clue can be found in the fact that many small businesses used the 2010 'holiday' in employer NI contributions not to hire extra staff but to give a pay rise to existing employees. In other words, the cut in employer NI actually benefited wages directly. This finding suggests a different model of wage and labour market reform: namely, formally linking progressive cuts in employer NI to wage increases. Higher wages both incentivise workers and reduce the Treasury bill for tax credits and in-work welfare payments. Osborne seemed to grasp this obvious logic – sort of – when he introduced the so-called National Living Wage in 2015. His ostensible aim was to force employers to raise wages – which is laudable. Unfortunately, his real intent was to disguise a massive cut to tax credits, with the result that many low-paid workers will actually be worse off. At the same time, employers in the private sector may actually lay off staff in order to keep the total wage bill static.

What we actually need is a way of restructuring NI contributions to incentivise employers to hire more workers – but at the same time not reducing public revenues. Banding rates more effectively would create incentives for firms to hire but ensure the Treasury does not lose out from unnecessary cuts in NI from higher-paid workers. Signalling in advance to employers that their NI contributions bill is going to be cut significantly according to a set timetable would also encourage prior investment and (therefore) hiring. Alternatively, we could focus policy on those sectors where low pay is most prevalent. The three obvious are social care, hospitality and wholesale and retail. One idea would be to re-introduce some form of Wages Boards in these areas to synchronise wage increases with focused NI cuts.

Rediscovering wage regulation

Wage boards to regulate remuneration fairly used to be commonplace in the UK. They gradually died a death in the post-war period as strong trades unions ensured wages kept pace with inflation and productivity. Indeed, the era of militant trades unions resulted in workers as a group increasing their share of National Income. Thatcherism and Reaganism put paid to that, of course. Neo-liberalism also killed off most of the remaining wage boards. The Agricultural Wage Board in England was finally abolished in 2013. However, Scotland and Wales have retained their own wage boards. The Scottish Agricultural Wages Board is an Executive Non-Departmental Public Body which sets minimum rates of pay, and holiday and sick pay entitlement, for agricultural workers. Both the National Union of Farmers and Unite are represented on the board. Let's experiment by extending the wage board system to other sectors where workers are poorly paid and have limited industrial muscle.

What a quaint idea, I hear the critics say. Not compatible with free-market capitalism and economic efficiency, they bellow. Yet there is one major capitalist economy where wage boards still play a powerful role yet the economy has not crumbled; namely, the United States. Ever since the Great Depression era, New York state has used wage boards to review pay and conditions for workers in a whole host of sectors, from beauty shops to summer camps. Convened by a commissioner appointed by the New York state governor, these wage boards are made up of representatives from labour, business and the general public. Their recommendations become law if approved by the commissioner. Recently, the panel regulating New York's fast-food sector caused a stir when it recommended a big rise in the minimum hourly rate for restaurant workers, to $15 an hour. This encouraged protests by fast-food workers across America, demanding similar action locally. In response, Seattle and San Francisco both passed laws raising their minimum wage to $15.

Back to the future: Selective Employment Tax

However, there is more to wage regulation than setting a minimum wage level. It is possible to use statutory wage legislation in a strategic direction to determine the shape of economic expansion. It has been done before.

The most radical post-war intervention in the UK labour market involved Selective Employment Tax, or SET, introduced in 1966. This was the brainchild of Harold Wilson's economic advisor, Nicky Kaldor. SET was a weekly payroll tax levied on all employers at a flat rate of £2.50 for males and (unjustifiable neither then nor now) half that for female workers. The purpose of SET was to subsidise manufacturing wage costs, particularly to lower exports costs. At the end of each accounting period, manufacturing companies had their SET payments refunded, along with a 75 pence bounty per employee. Effectively, service companies were subsidising manufacturing ones. SET was later abolished by the Heath administration in the early 1970s. Kaldor's thesis was that in an advanced industrial economy the less productive service sector tended to 'soak up' labour. Raising the cost of service sector labour relative to that in manufacturing, he argued, would increase average productivity. It would also provide a subsidy to manufacturing exporters and, by easing the balance of payments, make it possible to run the economy at a higher level of demand and so raise growth. A variation on SET was the Regional Employment Premium, or REP. This operated in a similar fashion, subsidising wage costs in areas of high unemployment, designated Development Areas. In part, they were meant to offset the negative impact on jobs of capital subsidies. REP operated as the equivalent to an exchange rate decrease, making a region's exports relatively cheaper. REP was abolished in 1977. At the time, the Scottish CBI estimated this led to a loss of 10,000 manufacturing jobs, while the independent Cambridge Institute of Applied Economics estimated a loss of about 14,000 jobs.

Both SET and REP had their problems but they are worth celebrating as the sort of bold experiments we need today. That raises the idea that we could price individual labour markets in a similar fashion in order to shift labour into desired, socially productive areas. One sector where there is certain to be a growing demand for labour over the next decades is caring. It is hardly worth stating that wages in this important sector are notoriously low, despite the high (often unmet) demand and desperate need for higher skills. Once again we see the conventional model of labour market economics fails us. The low pay of carers is not a function of their market abundance – so-called bed blocking in many local authority areas is a direct function of a scarcity of care staff. What we need to do is overcome social stereotypes regarding caring as a profession, and remove institutional and bureaucratic barriers to paying carers significantly more. We could do that via a statutory minimum wage for the sector, as discussed above. Or we could follow the SET/REP route and, say, impose a payroll levy on the financial sector to subsidise wages for carers.

The productivity dilemma

None of this discussion regarding Active Labour Market intervention should blind us to a real dilemma: there is indeed a causal link between what we can pay ourselves and economic productivity. My criticism of mainstream economics is that it locates this relationship at the level of the individual worker. Actually, the main, it lies at the level of the economy as a whole. It is national and sectoral investment in technology, infrastructure and skills that dictates productivity and productivity growth. Where the individual adds to productivity is through their creativity and skill. Can we find a way of tapping into individual human 'capital'?

Put another way: how do we create jobs which are both labour intensive yet highly productive, in order to substantiate high wages? Footballers cannot be replaced with machines. They also attract large paying audiences with their ball skills and entertainment value. Unfortunately, there are only a few thousand professional football stars and not everyone has the talent to be one (even if most males wish otherwise). Yet it certainly is the case that all of us have talents: performing, writing, making music, designing, creating gardens, knitting, clothes designing, writing computer games and apps, storytelling, making films and videos, building walls, and more. In fact, the list of marketable or exchangeable cultural skills is literally as long as the human imagination wants it to be. Because we value cultural products and skills highly, they can easily command a high return. Perhaps by encouraging individuals to seek work in the cultural field (widely defined) we can start to generate the labour intensive yet high wage employment required. And overcome the alienation of waged labour.

The immediate rejoinder is that most cultural jobs are not highly paid. Nor do they provide continuous employment – making films or performing music or plays tends to be a discontinuous activity. Famously, most aspirant actors in Hollywood are working in coffee bars. However, there is an employment model that turns this problem into an advantage and provides a mechanism to support large numbers of new entrants into the cultural industries. In France, people working in arts and entertainment – from circus clowns to camera operators – have a special dole system, designed to protect them in the down-time between paid jobs. Uniquely in France, out-of-work creatives do not have to wait tables or do telesales. The scheme is known as the intermittents du spectacle system, or IDS. Under IDS, a registered cultural worker – producer, actor, or technician – is automatically entitled to generous unemployment benefit provided they have worked for a total of 507 hours in the previous ten and a half months. Over 100,000 creative workers benefit from IDS. It is funded by employers and workers' contributions topped up by the state.

The great advantage of IDS is that it enables cultural workers and technicians to focus on their profession. Crucially, IDA is still paid if the worker is attending a training scheme, which means they can develop skills between professional contracts. IDS is one explanation of why France has the biggest cinema industry in Europe. There are other cultural benefits. For example, small theatre companies that can't pay for all rehearsals might pay the 507 hours, knowing the rest would be picked up in unemployment benefits. Most important from our perspective, IDS operates as a state subsidy which attracts young people into the creative industries and supports them during their training and career development. The demand for these creatives is (effectively) open-ended while the productivity gains to the economy are substantial. Plus there are few significant barriers of class, race, gender or basic education that would limit people trying to enter the cultural field of their choice. It is easy to see how such a scheme could be adopted in the UK, or in Scotland. It might be considered in due course by the Scottish Government as it develops its own plans for a separate welfare benefits agency.

Of course there are downsides to IDS. It suffers from frequent complaints that the administration is over bureaucratic. There are also persistent allegations that people 'buy' hours from production companies or from other technicians to make their employed time, if they are falling short of qualifying. Nor is IDS costless to the general taxpayer. Since the global recession and the Euro crisis, the funding deficit has reached €1bn, prompting calls for reform. On the other hand, the French budget gains because it does not have to provide more direct cultural subsidies, knowing that the unemployment insurance system will support creatives. IDS also underpins France's booming cultural export market. However, my suggestion here is not that we should replicate the French IDS exactly. It is rather that the general model could work as a way of subsidising employment in certain sectors without diminishing incentives to work, and at the same time boosting productivity more generally.

There is already a programme in Scotland to create new job opportunities and apprenticeships in the cultural sector for young people, especially from outside the middle class. This is fronted by the Scottish end of the UK-wide National Skills Academy for Creative & Cultural industries. This in turn is one of a cluster of public-private partnerships funded by government to improve work-based learning in the key industrial sectors – a complex delivery structure that is as bewildering to participants and those to those it is supposed to aid. The various initiatives in Scotland have been launched with much media ballyhoo. However, the actual number of cultural apprenticeships created in Scotland since 2008 amounts to only 3,500 while the exact number of additional jobs is difficult to discern. The problem lies in the structure of the cultural industries themselves. When it comes to apprenticeship schemes and job creation, it may be a mistake to treat the highly diverse cultural sector – where small units and intermittent work contracts are common – as if it was the same as the engineering industry. The complexity of the cultural sector makes a centralised, top-down approach to job creation too bureaucratic and even patronising.

This is where a Scottish version of IDS might help. Essentially, the IDS approach empowers the cultural worker and the small employer. Training becomes demand-led rather than the artificial creation of the government (anxious to get young folk off the unemployment register) or of private training agencies living off the public purse. The continuity of income provided by IDS also lets young people enter the industry long term, rather than dropping out when their apprenticeship ends. Finally, the on-the-job training IDS supports is a better way of encouraging wider class access into cultural fields, particularly for those who left school with insufficient qualifications to go to university but who later discover a real talent in music, art, writing or film.

Reducing work time

The essence of capitalism is the commodification of labour time, which is the root of social and individual alienation. More prosaically, the stress of finding and keeping a job, of competing in the modern neoliberal skilled labour market, and of surviving in today's regimented employment regime, is a major cause of the rise in mental health problems in late capitalism. How do we regain human control over work?

Can we find ways of reducing work time while enriching human existence, and at a cost that is not prohibitive and which does not reduce economic efficiency, given we are still living in a capitalist world? The Jimmy Reid Foundation has published an imaginative proposal for a phased introduction of a legally enforced 30-hour week.[7] One issue with this proposal is that we first need to improve the wage share (not just redistribute existing incomes) if we are to provide a decent living standard to low pay workers in low-productivity, service jobs. Second, it is not as simple as the authors suggest to divide up existing work hours between full and part time workers. Third, the pace at which Scotland can reduce the workweek depends on how fast similar reforms occur elsewhere in the world – as the negative French experience shows. That is not to say we should not consider tougher legal restraints on work hours. But it also suggests we might look for additional (and creative) strategies that can be introduced more quickly.

One experimental approach to reducing work time immediately, and coping with the problem that the normal workweek is difficult to reduce for full-time workers, is use of the sabbatical, or a lengthy period of leave at a reduced wage. A typical pay scale for sabbaticals is three-month leave at 50 per cent pay or 12-month leave at 20 per cent pay. To be useful to the worker, sabbaticals should be more than just holidays. For instance, social sabbaticals involve sending employees into emerging economies in support of local companies, NGOs and government agencies, with the aim of providing training and expertise. The employee on such a social sabbatical gains from the practical experience. There is a debate regarding the appropriate period a sabbatical should last: some argue that a 12-month leave period is too long and results in a depletion of skills. One model would be a legally mandatory scheme in which all employers must offer (after an appropriate term of service) either a one month unpaid, unrestricted time off, or three to six months off to pursue career development or volunteerism. This would be remunerated at a proportion of base salary. For administrative ease, employers could pay into a national fund. This could be supplemented by public funds, released by the likely reduction in benefit payments (such as Jobseeker's Allowance) resulting from the overall reduction in joblessness. There would also be economic and social benefits accruing from the lower human stress and greater skills resulting from the sabbaticals. In fact, mandatory sabbaticals could prove the single most revolutionary response Scotland could pioneer in order to reduce the standard capitalist working week.

Another approach to filling human time that is not determined by the capitalist labour market is some national Scottish scheme for public service, either at home or abroad. The United States has the Peace Corps and in the UK there is Voluntary Service Overseas, which has sent some 50,000 volunteers abroad since 1958. Jim Sillars has suggested a variation on this theme: a voluntary Scottish Overseas Service, linked to activity aboard a hospital ship. However, the idea being proposed here is akin to national military service, in that every young Scottish citizen would serve an appropriate period (possibly a year). The aim would be to mix the social classes, ensure every young person has contributed to the national good and provide leadership training. The upfront cost would be significant, but the social savings in subsequent years in reduced delinquency and alienation would offset the impact on the public purse. Training would be provided by a core of full time staff supplemented by adult 'reservists' recalled to service for temporary periods. Assuming a standard attachment of nine months to a year, the Scottish Peace Corps would probably have some 50,000 young people active at any one time. That's a large number to organise, but less than the 85,000 who regularly attend the T in the Park rock concerts. Mobilising 50,000 young people would provide a major social resource. Just think what we could do with it.

Socialising investment

The preceding discussion centred on stopping excess capital flows from causing harm through regular asset bubbles, and capturing a greater share of the social surplus for labour through increased employment. Can we go further and remove the impetus to capital accumulation for its own sake? Assuming we can't abolish capitalism overnight, far less instantly on a global scale, what can we do to socialise investment?

The conventional, social democratic answer is to encourage longer term investment rather than chasing the instant (often illusory) returns beloved of the investment market. A publicly-owned investment bank is one obvious route to achieving this, though it runs the risk of political favouritism and excess risk-taking underwritten by the taxpayer. Yet for a small country like Scotland, with a need to raise the level of productive investment in manufacturing, this route is certainly worth experimenting with. The SNP Government has already created a prototype Scottish Investment Bank, though it recently abandoned plans for a separate and parallel Business Development Bank. The SIB, which is a branch of Scottish Enterprise, is less an investment bank and more of a fund. In 2014–15, it invested £66.5 million in 155 local firms. That's very useful but is on a relatively small scale. A genuine bank would be able to tap the financial markets for the billions necessary to affect the shape and performance of the economy over the long term.

We will be told such a move is a threat to the free market and is tantamount to closet socialism. However, some of the most successful industrial nations have understood the need to impose rules favouring long term investment at the expense of asset bubbles. Take Germany, for instance, where there is a state-owned investment bank called the Kreditanstalt für Wiederaufbau (KfW), or Reconstruction Credit Institute. It was formed in 1948 as part of the Marshall Plan. KfW is owned jointly by the Federal Republic (80 per cent) and individual German states (20 per cent). In 2009, KfW lent £46bn to the German domestic market, mainly for infrastructure and green energy investment. That's roughly the magnitude required each year in the UK to finance needed energy infrastructure. KfW also invests in municipal infrastructure such as public transport and sanitation. KfW covers most of its borrowing needs in the ordinary capital markets, mainly through bonds guaranteed by the federal government. It is not allowed to compete unfairly with the private sector – a sensible provision. Instead, KfW provides commercial banks with liquidity at low rates and long maturities. Effectively, KfW provides cheaper, secure funds in partnership with private banks focused on strategic areas favoured by the Federal and state governments. Such a model could easily be adopted in Scotland. Actually, it already has been in the form of the Green Investment Bank (GIB), which has its corporate headquarters in Edinburgh. Here is an example of a public bank, founded with public money, which has pursued a strategy of long term investment in environmentally friendly infrastructure projects – and made a profit. Unfortunately, George Osborne decreed its privatisation in 2015 in order to raise cash for the Treasury.

How could any such a bank be capitalised initially by the Scottish Government or local authorities? Begin with the fact that the devolved authorities – Holyrood, local authorities, NHS and other agencies – already own substantial capital assets. According to a report prepared by Audit Scotland, devolved public sector bodies in Scotland had total capital assets valued at approximately £86 billion as at March 2012. Local government alone had £38 billion of assets in 2014, according to the Accounts Commission 2014. That is a substantial asset base. It would be perfectly possible to transfer ownership of some or all of these capital assets to the existing Scottish Investment bank, to act as collateral for raising funds in the market. That would give the SIB genuine economic clout.

But to do what with? The usual refrain from public investment bodies is of a lack of viable projects to fund. Actually, this is evidence the investment bank lacks imagination. A socialist, green or social democratic Scotland swimming in a capitalist sea has to take command of its own economic future. An effective state investment bank is a leader not a follower, especially in a small country. Consider the successful examples of Estonia and Israel. Both are tiny economies by global standards. Both lack natural resources, barring brains and entrepreneurial spirit. But each decided to carve out a global niche in high technology. They did so by pumping in investment cash backed by state orders in the first instance, to create the market. Their example proves that specialisation in high value added industry, backed by the willingness of the public authorities to underwrite some of the risk, can be transformative. Unfortunately, in Scotland we make two mistakes. First, we spread the investment funds across too many sectors: specialisation is the key to success. Second, we are still unambitious regarding the amount of public pump-priming we are prepared to envisage.

The crucial lesson to learn in creating a new public investment bank is that it must forge relationships directly with companies. The weakness in previous attempts at industrial policy is that they have focused on so-called (and vague) 'strategic sectors' rather than on energetic and entrepreneurial companies. It is also important for public investment to be 'mission-oriented'; that is focused on encouraging companies to bid for funds to solve specific social or industrial problems rather than 'creating new technologies' at a general level. This latter orientation was the Achilles Heel of the Intermediary Technology Institutes (ITIs) set up by Scottish Enterprise in 2003 with much fanfare and then scrapped in 2009 when they failed to generate significant new commercial patents. Government can lead by specifying the problem to be 'solved' and then fund companies to solve it. Government, on the other hand, should stay out of the way of saying how technological problems should be resolved at an engineering level. A mission-oriented funding approach is what creates markets and grows companies. But it takes time. The fundamental role of the investment bank is to give firms the time and latitude they need to solve technical problems and make them market ready.

Making capitalism obsolete?

In the end though, public investment banks still live within the parameters of financial risk and gain determined by the laws of capital accumulation. The experiment I am proposing here is not the crude state direction of investment but genuine socialisation of investment flows. I am not talking about greater market regulation (as the Labour Party proposed to do with the energy utilities in its 2015 general election manifesto) or correcting market 'defects'. I am talking about democratising the market economy itself. That means providing broader access to productive resources and opportunities currently 'owned' by the capitalist class. As we argued above, capitalism is not and never has been synonymous with markets or trading. Humans have always exchanged the fruits of their labour and will do so when capitalism is long gone. Uniquely, capitalism subverts the voluntary exchange of useful products and services (what Marx termed 'use values'). It does this by separating the worker (or groups of workers) from direct control of the means of production, and turning the exchange-market process into a sausage machine for creating and expanding capital itself. We need to give producers direct control over the means of production so they can produce and trade with others.

One suggestion for doing this comes from the American political philosopher David Schweickart.[8] In his model, firms and factories are 'communally' owned but rented and managed by worker cooperatives or social enterprises. These enterprises compete in markets to sell their goods with accounting profits (if any) shared by the workers. Each enterprise is taxed and that tax re-distributed via publicly owned banks, which fund expansion of new industry. This tax may be regarded as a capital leasing fee. The tax is passed on to consumers, so that all pay it, but in proportion to consumption. The capital assets tax is a surrogate interest rate. In Schweickart's model, these public banks are required to allocate investment funds to geographic regions on an equal per capita basis. Workers in an enterprise are free to organise production in any way they see fit. That covers what they produce, how they produce it, and what they charge for their products in the marketplace. Entrepreneurship and skill still drive productivity gains and still respond to consumer choice. These worker-run enterprises exist in a genuine market economy, so they must compete with other enterprises. The incomes of all workers are profit shares, not wages, so all are motivated to organise production efficiently. The enterprise is obligated to maintain a depreciation fund so that the value of those assets under their control is maintained.

In Schweickart's model, business credit is abolished, there are no stocks or bonds, and private capital accumulation is eliminated. We need not ban the investment of private savings, which could be used to purchase assets for personal use – building your own home – or channelled into pure consumer loans. However, the social role of private finance would be small, because capital investment is socialised. As a result, the expansion path of the economy will no longer depend on the (uncertain) expectation of a return on financial assets. Expansion is thus more sustainable and linked to real productivity growth rather than speculation or debt-fuelled conspicuous consumption. In the unlikely event there are insufficient opportunities for productive expansion of capacity, a portion of the social investment fund could be returned to the firms who paid the capital tax, who would then distribute it to their workers. That automatically boosts effective demand for new productive capacity. Efficiency is still tested by the market but the direction and pace of 'growth' is hitched to genuine need rather than autonomous capital accumulation.

Schweickart's is a utopian model but aspects of it could be appropriated as an experiment within a capitalist economy. Some on the left have rejected his ideas, arguing that the market is an integral component of capitalism. Manifestly and historically, it is not. Besides, the negative experience with central planning shows that some other form of economic coordinating mechanism is required – and that can only be through some market search system. A more telling critique of Schweickart is that it assumes a total replacement of the capitalist model (inside a single nation or region) to work. Achieving that is problematic. More likely, we would have to launch a limited version initially, running alongside a capitalist (and capital accumulating) sector. Even then, we would need to start with enough participating 'democratic' enterprises to make the project viable. There is also the question of meeting legal challenges from the capitalist sector for alleged infringements of EU subsidy rules. The latter is not an insurmountable problem as, after all, the EU Commission regularly bends the rules to meet the exigencies demanded by member states. The Commission happily agreed to the UK Government's insane (even by capitalist accounting methods) subsidies of EDF's Hinkley Point C nuclear plant.

By way of a conclusion

The foregoing, and the other contributions to this book, are by way of an opening gambit in creating a new Scottish political economy. I make no claims to providing a definitive critique of contemporary capitalism, or to provide sure fire alternatives. This is a plea for fresh thinking and a more experimental attitude to policy-making. The real essence of Marx's dialectical approach is that colliding with reality not only changes the problem, it must thereby make us change our ideas, or condemn once-progressive thinking to sterile ideology.

Which brings me to perhaps my greatest heresy, though one John Maynard Keynes made (and he was in essence the saviour of capitalism, in his day). If global deflation has set in, with prices spiralling downwards for the next couple of decades, we will need radical state economic intervention to reverse course. For small nations like Scotland, that could call into question the dominant paradigm of untrammelled free trade. Open economies have brought much good but also much evil. Do not forget that the British invented the doctrine of free trade in order to force the Chinese to accept our opium production (based in India). In order to reflate domestically, small nations like Scotland will require a degree of protection, or see aggregate demand flow abroad. Provided we use such protection wisely in order to create world class firms – as the Nordic countries did in the 1950s and 1960s – it would be possible to offset higher domestic costs by charging a premium for our exports. Of course, a Scotland still inside the UK would not have this flexibility. Nor, indeed, would any member of the European Union. However, I remain sceptical that the free trade model (including the free movement of capital) will survive the strains and stresses of a deflationary global economy.

I only raise this issue, in such a trivial form, to underscore the need for unconventional thinking when it comes to taming the capitalist beast. After all, that is precisely the intellectual journey embarked upon by a certain Adam Smith back in 1776.[9]

A post-Brexit epilogue

The rapidity of political and economic change often plays havoc with publishing schedules. I wrote the above substantially in the months before the 2015 Westminster General Election. It represented a working-through and break with some of my earlier positions, in the light of the 2007 banking crisis. A few minor amendments to the original text were made after George Osborne's so-called emergency budget in July 2015. Since then we have witnessed a veritable political revolution: a surprise Brexit referendum, the defenestration of the Cameron administration (along with Chancellor Osborne) and the re-election of a third SNP administration at Holyrood. Above all, the prospect of a second independence referendum is back on the agenda. Nevertheless, the core analysis presented in this section remains valid: Western capitalism in its contemporary, neoliberal model is non-viable. Permanent, structural income inequalities are undermining democracy and giving rise to dangerous populist movements of the kind that provoked the Brexit vote in the UK and the rise of Donald Trump in the United States. A glut of capital is leading to reckless financial speculation via a banking system that remains largely unreformed since the excesses of the first decade of the century. Yet mainstream political economy remains fundamentally incapable of describing an escape path.

My own central conclusions remain broadly the same: greater socialisation of capital investment decisions and a determined effort to explore radical, human-centred alternatives in deciding resource and labour allocation. I remain convinced this experimentation is most fruitfully conducted in a small economy and communitarian society such as Scotland. Indeed, the first stage in this new thinking is presaged by the decision (in September 2015) of First Minister Nicola Sturgeon to appoint a free-thinking commission of academics, entrepreneurs and elected members tasked with finding ways in which Scotland's economic growth can be stimulated in the wake of the Brexit vote. Let's hope they read this book.

Notes

1   Roberto Unger, *What Should the Left Propose?*, Verso 2005. For Unger, a political programme is not a utopian blueprint but a

direction. Unger draws on the rich experience with urban social experimentation in Latin America. Anyone interested in my own analysis of the Scottish economy, by way of background to this piece, should see George Kerevan and Alan Cochrane, *Scottish Independence: Yes or No*, The History Press 2014

2   For a thorough analysis of the data see Engelbert Stockhamme, 'Why have wage shares fallen?' in *Conditions of Work and Employment* Series No. 35, ILO 2013

3   Carl Benedikt Frey and Michael A. Osborne, 'The Future of Employment: How susceptible are jobs to computerisation?' in Oxford Martin School Papers, September 2013

4   For Keynes' arguments in favour of an annual wealth tax, or 'capital levy', see John Maynard Keynes, *Collected Writings* Volume XXVII, Royal Economic Society 1980

5   See James Mirrlees (ed.), *Tax By Design: The Mirrlees Review*, Institute for Fiscal Studies 2012. Mirrlees is a Nobel Prize winner and a member of the SNP Government's Fiscal Commission

6   Thomas Piketty, *Capital in the Twenty-First Century*, Harvard University Press 2014. 8. P. Kane, I. Lindsay, G. Wales, B. Wray, *Time for Life*, Jimmy Reid Foundation April 2014

7   P. Kane, I. Lindsay, G. Wales, B. Wray, *Time for Life*, Jimmy Reid Foundation April 2014

8   David Schweickart, After Capitalism, Rowman & Littlefield 2002

9   For those interested in reading more about the relevance of Adam Smith to the contemporary crisis of capitalism, see Giovanni Arrighi, *Adam Smith in Beijing*, Verso 2007. This tour de force deserves more recognition that Piketty's work

A Utopia like any other: Inside the Swedish Model

Dominic Hinde
ISBN: 978-1-910745-32-8 PB £7.99

Does a utopia really exist within northern Europe? Do we have anything to learn from it if it does? And what makes a nation worthy of admiration, anyway?

Since the '30s, when the world was wowed by the Stockholm Exhibition, to most people Sweden has meant clean lines, good public housing, and a Social Democratic government. More recently the Swedes have been lauded for their environmental credentials, their aspirational free schools, and their hardy economy. But what's the truth of the Swedish model? Is modern Sweden really that much better than rest of Europe?

In this insightful exploration of where Sweden has been, where it's going, and what the rest of us can learn from its journey, journalist Dominic Hinde explores the truth behind the myth of a Swedish Utopia. In his quest for answers Hinde travels the length of the country and beyond: enjoying July sunshine on the island of Gotland for 'Almedalan Week'; venturing into the Arctic Circle to visit a town about to be swallowed up by the very mine it exists to serve; even taking a trip to Shanghai to take in the suburban Chinese interpretation of Scandinavia, 'Sweden Town', a Nordic city in miniature in the smog of China's largest city.

Caledonian Dreaming
The Quest for a Different Scotland

GERRY HASSAN
with a foreword by Finton O'Toole
ISBN: 978-1-910021-32-3 RPB £11.99

Caledonian Dreaming: The Quest for a Different Scotland offers a penetrating and original way forward for Scotland beyond the current independence debate. It identifies the myths of modern Scotland, describes what they say and why they need to be seen as myths. Hassan argues that Scotland is already changing, as traditional institutions and power decline and new forces emerge, and outlines a prospectus for Scotland to become more democratic and to embrace radical and far-reaching change.

Hassan drills down to deeper reasons why the many dysfunctions of British democracy could dog an independent Scotland too. With a non-partisan but beady eye on society both sides of the border, in this clever book here are tougher questions to consider than a mere Yes/No.
POLLY TOYNBEE, *The Guardian*

A brilliant book unpacking the political narratives that have shaped modern Scotland in order to create a space to imagine anew. A book about Scotland important to anyone, anywhere, dreaming a new world.
STEPHEN DUNCOMBE, *Author*

Luath Press Limited
committed to publishing well written books worth reading

LUATH PRESS takes its name from Robert Burns, whose little collie Luath (*Gael.*, swift or nimble) tripped up Jean Armour at a wedding and gave him the chance to speak to the woman who was to be his wife and the abiding love of his life. Burns called one of 'The Twa Dogs' Luath after Cuchullin's hunting dog in Ossian's *Fingal*. Luath Press was established in 1981 in the heart of Burns country, and now resides a few steps up the road from Burns' first lodgings on Edinburgh's Royal Mile. Luath offers you distinctive writing with a hint of unexpected pleasures.

Most bookshops in the UK, the US, Canada, Australia, New Zealand and parts of Europe either carry our books in stock or can order them for you. To order direct from us, please send a £sterling cheque, postal order, international money order or your credit card details (number, address of cardholder and expiry date) to us at the address below. Please add post and packing as follows: UK – £1.00 per delivery address; overseas surface mail – £2.50 per delivery address; overseas airmail – £3.50 for the first book to each delivery address, plus £1.00 for each additional book by airmail to the same address. If your order is a gift, we will happily enclose your card or message at no extra charge.

Luath Press Limited
543/2 Castlehill
The Royal Mile
Edinburgh EH1 2ND
Scotland
Telephone: 0131 225 4326 (24 hours)
email: sales@luath.co.uk
Website: www.luath.co.uk